WÄLDER DER ERDE   **FORESTS OF THE WORLD**

WÄLDER DER ERDE

EINE FOTOGRAFISCHE SAMMLUNG
FÜR UNSERE ZUKUNFT

IDEE UND REALISATION
HEINRICH GOHL

FORESTS OF THE WORLD

A PHOTOGRAPHIC COLLECTION
FOR OUR FUTURE

CREATED BY
HEINRICH GOHL

WÄLDER DER ERDE

FORESTS OF THE WORLD

19. August 2007 bis 6. Januar 2008

FONDATION **BEYELER**

INHALT

CONTENTS

Heinrich Gohl (1926)
Cook Inlet, Nikishka Küste
Alaska/USA, September 1998

Heinrich Gohl (1926)
Cook Inlet, Nikishka Coast
Alaska/USA, September 1998

ZUM GELEIT

Wenn ein Bild imstande ist, mehr als tausend Worte zu sagen, dann nutzen wir die Kraft der Bilder. Dann sollen sie die Erinnerung daran wachrufen, dass unsere Vorfahren den Wald heiligten, dass der Baum Lebenssymbol war. In der nordischen Mythologie trägt und umfasst der Weltbaum, die Weltesche «Yggdrasill», die Schöpfung. Und bis auf den Tag hätte wohl kein Republikaner etwas dagegen, Bäume königlich, Wälder majestätisch zu nennen.

Die Ausstellung «Wälder der Erde» soll Erinnerung an Schönheit und Würde der Natur sein. Sie soll Lockung sein und Mahnung des Menschen, den Friedensvertrag mit der Natur zu erfüllen, wie ihn der Künstler Friedensreich Hundertwasser 1986 aufsetzte: «Die Schöpfung des Menschen (Kunst) und die Schöpfung der Natur müssen wiedervereinigt werden».

Liesse Lyrik sich als Kurzschrift der Vernunft begreifen? Dann machen drei Zeilen aus einem Sonett von Goethe deutlich, worum es geht:

> Und wenn wir erst in abgemessnen Stunden
> Mit Geist und Fleiss uns an die Kunst gebunden,
> Mag frei Natur im Herzen wieder glühen.

«Wälder der Erde» soll als Zeitzeugnis verstanden werden, das bleibt. Als Bildergalerie unberührter Wälder und ihrer Pracht. «Wälder der Erde» soll visuelles Inventar sein, das nicht nur die Nachwelt, sondern uns selber an das Schöpfungswunder Wald erinnert, an seine Schönheit und an unseren Auftrag, sie zu erhalten.

WWF International
General Director
James P Leape

Greenpeace International
General Director
Gerd Leipold

If a picture has the ability to speak more than a thousand words, then we should make use of the power of the image it presents. It should evoke memories of our forefathers worshipping the forests, that for them the tree was a symbol of life. In Nordic mythology the world tree carries and encircles the world ash tree "Yggdrasill", the whole universe. Till today, no republican would have any qualms in calling the tree kingly and the forest majestic.

The exhibition "Forests of the World" should be a reminder of the beauty and grace of nature. Its aim is to entice and warn humanity to fulfill its peace treaty once made with nature, as put by the artist Friedensreich Hundertwasser in 1986: "The creation of man (art) and the creation of nature must once again become as one".

Does lyric in its short form allow understanding of reason? If so, this can be made clear by three lines taken from the sonnet "Nature and Art" by Goethe:

> Devotion to our craft, unceasing practice
> With heart and mind; then only may we witness
> Nature kindle again as free as ever.

"Forests of the Earth" should be understood as a witness of the times that will remain with you forever. "Forests of the Earth" should be a visual inventory that not only our future world but also we should remember the wonder of creation "forest", its beauty, and our duty to up-keep it.

Fondation Beyeler
Ernst Beyeler

Stiftung Wald-Klima-Umwelt
Heinrich Gohl

FONDATION **BEYELER**

Heinrich Gohl (1926)
Everglades
Florida/USA, Februar 1983

Heinrich Gohl (1926)
Everglades
Florida/USA, February 1983

DANK

Zuallererst danke ich all den Fotografen, Rechtsnachfolgern und Mitarbeitern, die sich für die Idee begeistern liessen und mit ihren einzigartigen Aufnahmen das Gelingen der Ausstellung erst möglich machten. Ohne sie wäre nie ein so vielfältiges Bild über die Wälder unserer Erde entstanden.

Ohne die grosszügige finanzielle Unterstützung eines nicht genannt sein wollenden Mäzens hätte das Projekt nicht in dieser Form verwirklicht werden können. Vertrauen und Mut durften so entstehen.

Als Hauptsponsor engagierte sich die Bank Sarasin, Basel. Ihrem Unternehmensprofil getreu unterstützte sie mit ihrem grosszügigen Beitrag die Ausstellung und Felix Rudolf von Rohr begleitete das Projekt bei der Umsetzung und den flankierenden Massnahmen. Seine persönlichen Kontakte ebneten Wege, öffneten Türen und schafften so wichtige Verbindungen.

Ernst Beyeler ermöglichte mit der Zusage der Fondation Beyeler als Erstausstellungsort den Start in einem angesehenen Haus. Sein Engagement für die Rettung des Tropenwaldes ist Vorbild und Bestätigung. Christoph Vitali, Direktor der Fondation, zeigte sich spontan offen und schuf die Akzeptanz in der Institution.

Ulf Küster, Guido Magnaguagno und Reinhold Hohl gaben mit ihren Betrachtungen und Textbeiträgen der Botschaft der Ausstellung die entsprechende Form. Alexander Lukas Bieri verfasste die Biografien der Fotografen. Rolf Steinebrunner übersetzte die deutschen Texte ins Englische und führte die englische Korrespondenz. Albert Gomm gestaltete den Katalog in der vorliegenden Fassung.

Willy Mayer, Präsident der Karl Mayer Stiftung, unterstützte mit gutem Rat und vermittelte Verbindungen für zukünftige Ausstellungsorte. Aus dem Freundeskreis kam tatkräftige Unterstützung bei der Realisation des Kataloges. Ein ganz besonderer Dank gilt meiner Frau und meinen Kindern, die Geduld, Nachsicht und Verständnis für das alles in Anspruch nehmende Projekt aufbrachten. Während der gesamten Vorbereitungszeit konnte ich mich stets auf ihre konstruktiv kritische und wohlwollend hinterfragende Unterstützung verlassen.

Vielen herzlichen Dank euch allen!   Heinrich Gohl

ACKNOWLEDGEMENT

First of all, I would like to thank all the photographers, legal successors and staff members who allowed themselves to get excited about the project and who, with their unique photographs, made this exhibition possible. Without them it would not have been possible to come up with such manifold images of the forests of the earth.

Without the generous financial support by a person who wishes to be treated anonymously, the project could not have been realized in this way. Confidence and courage could thus become reality.

As the main sponsor, the Bank Sarasin, Basel, engaged itself true to its corporate profile supported the exhibition with a generous contribution and Felix Rudolf von Rohr accompanied the project by enforcing its implementation and the accompanying measures. His personal contacts paved ways, opened doors and thus created important connections.

Ernst Beyeler made it possible that the Fondation Beyeler agreed to let the exhibition start its tour at his prestigious house. His engagement for the preservation of the tropical forests is an example and confirmation of his generosity. Christoph Vitali, director of the Foundation, proved to be spontaneously open to the idea and created acceptance at the institution.

Ulf Küster, Guido Magnaguagno and Reinhold Hohl with their evaluation and written contributions gave the message of the exhibition its proper form. Alexander Lukas Bieri wrote the biographies of the photographers. Rolf Steinebrunner translated the German texts into English and conducted the English correspondence. Albert Gomm designed the catalogue in its present version.

Willy Mayer, president of the Karl Mayer Stiftung, gave his support with good counsel and arranged connections for future exhibition sites. The realization of the catalogue was due to the active support of my circle of friends.

Lastly, a special thank you goes to my wife and my children who, with patience, forbearance and understanding, supported me throughout this all-demanding project. I was always able to count on them for constructive critical and meaningful considerations during the entire planning stage.

My most cordial thanks go to all of you!   Heinrich Gohl

Eine der schönsten Beschreibungen des Waldes ist in Friedrich Schillers grossartigem Gedicht «Der Spaziergang» von 1794, einem wahren Wortgemälde, zu finden. Im Mittelpunkt des Geschehens steht der Mensch, der in einer Art «Tour de Force» einen sich «schlängelnden Pfad» verfolgt, von dem aus er Landschaften sieht, die ihn zu verschiedenen Reflexionen, zu Erkenntnis und Selbsterkenntnis führen. Hier ein kleiner Ausschnitt:

> Doch jetzt brausts aus dem nahen Gebüsch, tief neigen der Erlen
> Kronen sich, und im Wind wogt das versilberte Gras,
> Mich umfängt ambrosische Nacht; in duftende Kühlung
> Nimmt ein prächtiges Dach schattender Buchen mich ein,
> In des Waldes Geheimnis entflieht mir auf einmal die Landschaft,
> Und ein schlängelnder Pfad leitet mich steigend empor.

Der plötzliche Eintritt in den Wald lässt die Landschaft in das «Geheimnis des Waldes» entfliehen, wie Schiller so schön schreibt. Wie ist das zu verstehen? Was bedeutet hier «Landschaft», was «Wald» und dessen «Geheimnis»? Landschaft war für Schiller eindeutig noch ein Bild, und zwar das Bild, das sich der Mensch von der Natur macht. Schiller hat noch sehr genau zwischen den Begriffen Natur und Landschaft unterschieden; heute, und das ist nicht unproblematisch, wird Landschaft oft mit Natur gleichgesetzt. Auch der Begriff Natur wird in Schillers Gedicht «Der Spaziergang» erwähnt. Natur ist aber für ihn, und eigentlich gilt dies bis heute, eher ein Prinzip als ein Zustand: Während Natur sich ständig ändert und überhaupt nur eine schwer zu beeinflussende Grösse ist, ist Landschaft ein von der Wahrnehmung des Menschen bestimmtes Konstrukt, das sich nicht ändert und das eine positive Bedeutung hat. Natur als Prinzip der Veränderung, als Leben, das den Tod einschliesst, wird bis heute als unentrinnbar und bedrohlich empfunden; Landschaft ist bis heute der Sehnsuchtsort, den es vor der Veränderung und damit, wenn man es ganz genau nimmt, sogar vor der Natur zu schützen gilt.

Auch der Begriff «Wald» ist im Sinne von Landschaft zu verstehen. Wir sehen, wenn wir «Wald» denken, ein bestimmtes Bild vor uns, das bestimmte Empfindungen auslöst. Dass Wald eine Ansammlung von Bäumen ist, die zusammen ein kompliziertes biologisches System bilden, welches sich durch Wachstum verändert und häufig durch den Menschen stark genutzt wird, sieht man eigentlich erst richtig, wenn man sich im Wald selbst aufhält. Dort sieht man nämlich meist «vor lauter Bäumen den Wald nicht», und das ist es wohl, was Schiller gemeint hat, als er schrieb, die Landschaft, in diesem Falle unser Bild vom Wald, «entfliehe», wenn man den Wald betritt. Möglicherweise ist dies auch das eigentliche «Geheimnis» des Waldes: Damit ist nämlich nicht nur unser Bild vom Wald als mit Erinnerungen, mit Mythen, mit Empfindungen aufgeladener Ort gemeint. Das Geheimnis des Waldes besteht auch darin, dass er gleichzeitig ein Teil der sich verändernden, dem Wachstum unterworfenen Natur ist, dass er lebenswichtiges Teil des Ökosystems

Fichten am Tayon Creek
Alaska/USA, Oktober 1967

Spruces, Tayon Creek
Alaska/USA, October 1967

Fichtenwald
Bödmern/Schweiz, August 1989

Spruce forest
Bödmern/Switzerland, August 1989

Erde ist und, seitdem es den Menschen gibt, für diesen Wirtschaftsraum bedeutet, weil man sich die Natur des Waldes, das Wachstum von Holz, zunutze macht. Der Mensch ist somit in vielfacher Form mit dem Wald emotional und ganz praktisch verbunden, ja sogar von ihm abhängig.

Schiller schrieb sein Gedicht zur Zeit der beginnenden industriellen Revolution, während der ein Prozess der zunehmenden Entfremdung des Menschen von dem Wissen einsetzte, in die Veränderungszyklen der Natur eingebunden zu sein. Gleichzeitig wurde begonnen, massiv Energieressourcen auszubeuten, die – auf lange Sicht – liebgewordene Natur als Landschaft bedrohte. Dass der Mensch durch sein Dasein schon lange in natürliche Zyklen eingegriffen hatte, wurde zunehmend vergessen; übernutzte Landschaft wurde als Urlandschaft romantisiert. Bestes Beispiel ist die Lüneburger Heide, die nichts anderes als ein überweideter und seit der frühen Neuzeit versteppter, sogenannter Hütewald ist: Das Vieh wurde bis zur Revolutionierung der Landwirtschaft, also noch bis ins 20. Jahrhundert hinein, durch den Menschen auf die Weide in den Wald getrieben, was seine Spuren hinterlassen hat.

Seit dem 18. Jahrhundert ist der Wunsch gross, die Landschaft, also das jeweilige Bild von der Natur, zu schützen, sei es als tatsächlicher Ort oder als Bild in Form eines Gemäldes. Vielleicht sind die schönsten Zeugnisse da-

von die Bilder Caspar David Friedrichs, die für viele heute Urbilder des Waldes darstellen, obwohl fast ausschliesslich auf ihnen Bäume zu sehen sind, die deutlich die Nutzung durch den Menschen zeigen.

Man sollte bei der Betrachtung der wunderbaren Fotografien vom Wald, die in der Ausstellung gezeigt werden, diese vielfältigen Beziehungen des Menschen mit dem Wald immer bedenken. Zu sehen sind Bilder, die sich der Mensch vom Wald gemacht hat; ihre Verwandtschaft mit den Werken Caspar David Friedrichs ist unverkennbar. Manche dieser Bilder zeigen sogar Wälder, die vom Menschen noch mehr oder weniger unberührt sind. Immer aber ist der Mensch dabei, und wenn «nur» als Fotograf, der die Aufnahme gemacht hat.

Über den Wald und unsere Beziehungen zu ihm können wir lernen, wie sehr wir Teil eines Ganzen sind, für das Sorge zu tragen ist. Dabei ist das Schützen von Landschaft, von unserem Bild, das wir von Natur haben, von gleich grosser Bedeutung wie verantwortliches Wirtschaften. Hildy und Ernst Beyeler, die die Stiftung Tropenwald ins Leben gerufen haben, die sich für den Erhalt eines wesentlichen Teils der «grünen Lunge» der Erde einsetzt, haben hier wieder einmal ein Beispiel gegeben. Es bleibt zu hoffen, dass viele Menschen durch die Ausstellung aufgerufen werden, das «Geheimnis des Waldes» und die sich daraus ergebende Verantwortung persönlich zu entdecken.
Ulf Küster

One of the most beautiful descriptions of the forest that one can find is Friedrich Schiller's marvellous poem "The Walk" of 1794, a true painting in words. In the centre of it stands the human being, who somehow in a "Tour de Force" follows a "serpentine path" from which he can see landscapes that lead him to various reflections, awareness and self-awareness. Here is a short excerpt:

> Now it roars in the bushes nearby, the crowns of the alders
> Bend deeply, and the wind waves through the silvery grass.
> Night ambros'al closes me round: in sweet-smelling freshness
> O'er me the shadowy birch join in sumptuous roof,
> In the secretive woods the landscape escapes me a moment,
> And a serpentine path climbing conducts me above.

The sudden entry into the forest allows the landscape to escape into "the secret of the woods", as Schiller so beautifully puts it. How may this be understood? What is the meaning of "landscape", what about "wood" and its "secret"? Clearly, landscape for Schiller was still a picture, a picture of nature which man pictures for himself. Schiller differentiated very much between the notion of nature and landscape; today, and this is not unproblematic as landscape is often put on a level with nature. The term nature is also mentioned in Schiller's poem "The Walk".

But rather, and this is still true today, nature for him is a principal rather than a condition. While nature is continuously changing, in hardly to be influenced dimensions, landscape in the perception of the human being is a construct designed by him that does not change and which has a positive meaning. Nature as a principal of change, as life, which includes death, is until today still conceived to be inescapable and menacing; landscape is a place of longing that needs to be protected from change and when one looks at it very closely, it even needs to be protected from nature.

Also, the term "Forest" is to be understood in the sense of landscape. When we think of "Forest", we form a defined picture in front of us which sets off defined sentiments. One is in fact only really aware of the fact that a wood is an accumulation of trees that together build a complex biological system that changes through growth and is often heavily used by humans when one stays in the woods itself. To wit, there "one cannot see the wood for the trees" and this may well be what Schiller meant in his writing; the landscape, in this instance our picture of the forest, "escapes" as one enters the forest.

Possibly, this may well be the "secret" of the forest: with which not only our picture of the forest with recollections and myths, a site charged with sentiments, is meant. The secret of the forest is also that it is an ever-changing part of nature, subject to growth that it is a vitally important piece of the world's ecosystem and, since man's existence, has been an economic area for him, since he is able to make use of the nature of the forest in that it grows wood. Hence, humans are tied emotionally and

Schwarzpappel
Rügen/Deutschland, August 2001

Black Poplar
Rügen/Germany, August 2001

Mangroven, Everglades
Florida/USA, März 1981

Mangroves, Everglades
Florida/USA, March 1981

practically to the forest in many ways, to the point of being dependent on it.

Schiller wrote his poem at the time of the industrial revolution during which a process of estrangement in the awareness of humans took place to be integrated in the ever-changing cycles of nature. At the same time, a massive exploitation of nature's resources began which – in the long run – endangered endearing landscapes as nature. Increasingly it was forgotten that the human presence had already been encroaching upon the natural cycles for a long time and the over-utilised landscapes had become romanticized. The best example is the Luneburg Heather landscape which as a result of over grazing in the early modern past has by desertification turned into nothing more than so-called pasture woodland: well into the 20th century, until agriculture was revolutionized, the cattle were driven by humans to pastures in the woods which has left its mark.

Since the 18th century there has been a great desire to protect the landscape, the particular picture of nature, be it as the actual place or in the form of a painting. Perhaps the most beautiful witnesses of these are the paintings by Caspar David Friedrich, which today for many portray ar-

chetype pictures of the forest, even though they almost exclusively display trees that clearly show use by humans. In looking at the wonderful photographs of the forest shown at the exhibition, one should always remember the manifold relationships man has had with the forest. To see are pictures that man has made of the forests; their unmistakable kinship can be seen especially in the works of Caspar David Friedrich. Many of the pictures even show forests that have more or less been left untouched by humans. Still, man is ever present, even if only as the photographer who took the picture.

By way of the forest and how we relate to it, we can learn just how much we are part of the whole and that we should take good care of it. In doing so, the protection of landscape and the picture we have of nature is of equal importance. Hildy and Ernst Beyeler, the founders of the foundation Tropenwald (Rain Forest), which is engaged in preserving a considerable portion of the "Green Lung" of the earth, have once again set an example. We can only hope that through this exhibition many people will be evoked by the "Secret of the Forest" and as a result will discover their personal responsibility for its well-being.   Ulf Küster

Am Sprichwort «Man sieht vor lauter Bäumen den Wald nicht» hat mich immer auch die Möglichkeit seiner Umkehrung fasziniert. Der Einzelne und die vielen. Und das Erlebnis einer vollendeten Einheit.

Wenn ich das «Musée imaginaire de la photographie» abschreite, begegnen mir von Anfang an akkurat beleuchtete Baumstämme von Adolphe Braun, Eugène Atget, Gustave Le Gray. Der Wald von Fontainebleau hat auch im neuen Bildmedium deutliche Spuren hinterlassen. Es stellen sich Bilder ein im Spätwerk von Paul Strand, Blätter nur, die in seinem letzten Album «On my doorstep» als pars pro toto die vegetabile Welt als Schöpfungsgleichnis feiern.

So ist «der Wald» in seiner ganzen Ausdehnung vom Allerkleinsten ins Riesengrosse ein unermessliches Thema der Fotografie, eine eigentliche zentrale Bildmetapher, so wie er in ökologischer Sicht für das Weltklima besorgt ist. Eine Art seismographisches Symbol.

Jeder Spaziergänger, jeder Wanderer verfügt über seine spezifischen Erinnerungsbilder. Häufig sind sie durch Erlebnisse in der Kindheit präfiguriert. Nie werde ich den frischen betäubenden Geruch vergessen, als ich jeweils samstags mit meinem appenzellischen Grossvater Wilhelm Weishaupt in sein eigenes Stück Tannenwald ausfliegen durfte, wo er die eben gefällten Bäume bis zu «Holzbürdeli» verarbeitete. Solche Bilder tauchten unmittelbar noch auf, als ich letzthin zu Henry David Thoreaus «Walden» pilgerte und den magischen Ort seiner Waldhütte und den von lichten Bäumen gesäumten «Pond» umkreiste. Hier roch ich die Düfte meiner Kindheit, James Fenimore Coopers «Lederstrumpf», und begriff über Zeit und Raum das Wachstum der pflanzlichen Welt. Ihre Seele.

In der noch immer kurzen Bildergeschichte der Fotografie, die voll ist von hervorragenden Zeugnissen eben-

solcher Augenblicke, begegnete offenbar nicht nur mir im Werk von Ansel Adams die tiefe Erfahrung des Wiedererkennens solcher Gefühle. Nur durch diese von allen teilbare Botschaft hat es seinen herausragenden Rang erworben und behauptet. Was dem technischen, kühlen und glatten Medium nur wenige Eingeweihte zugetraut hatten, wurde durch seine enorme Empathie und seine Fähigkeit, die Zeit gleichsam anzuhalten und den Bildgegenstand gestalterisch zu beschwören, zur Inkunabel. Als ich die kalifornischen Redwoods bestaunen durfte, sah ich sie mit den Augen des Ansel Adams. Dank sei ihm, dem «Trapper» der Fotogeschichte.

An ihm haben alle Jünger Mass genommen. Von seinem Bildersegen haben sich alle Neuerer abzusetzen. Wenn ich die Ausbeute abschätze, welche Heinrich Gohl für diese Publikation und die gleichnamige Ausstellung zusammengetragen hat, so ist sein Erbe lange und intensiv spürbar. Nichts ersetzt den gleichsam direkten «Zugriff», den Gang vors Modell, die Wanderschaft, das Abenteuer, gepaart mit Wissen, die Passion. Dieser Bildgegenstand überwältigt und lässt häufig nicht mehr los. Daubigny und Théodore Rousseau, der gewaltige Courbet und der ewige Cézanne lassen grüssen. Bonjour, neue, bedrohte Welt, samt weisem Max Ernst. Der Zauber des Unwiederbringlichen umfängt sie, ein Abgesang vor der vermuteten Zerstörung – Fotografie als Epitaph. Bilder als Beschwörungsforme(l)n. Dass Heinrich Gohl selber so eindrücklich eigentliche Urlandschaften gefunden und für uns aufbewahrt hat, macht ihn zum geeignetsten Fürsprecher eines Unternehmens, das der Welt den Atem erhält.

Wer hätte gedacht, dass Fotografie dazu beiträgt. Und dass jenes Papier, das auch sie dem Wald und seinen vielen Bäumen verdankt, nicht nach Silberoxyd riecht, sondern nach dem Tau eines zarten Fichtensprösslings.   Guido Magnaguagno

The saying "one cannot see the wood for the trees" always fascinated me because of its possibility to be turned around. The single and the many. And the experience of a complete unit.

As I pace along the "Musée imaginaire de la photographie", I immediately encounter accurately illuminated tree stems from Adolphe Braun, Eugène Atget, and Gustave Le Gray. The woods of Fontainebleau have also left their clear traces in the new medium of images. Pictures come into focus of the late works of Paul Strand, sheets only, but which celebrate in his last album "On my doorstep", as pars pro toto, the vegetable world as an analogy of creation.

Thus, "The Forest" in his entire dimension from the minute to the vast becomes an unfathomable topic in photography, in a sense a central image metaphor much like it is concerned about the world climate from the standpoint of ecology. Somehow a seismic symbol.

Each stroller, each hiker has access to his specific image memory. They are often prefixed in childhood experiences. I will never forget the fresh and intoxicating inhalation as I was able to take a trip out with my grandfather Wilhelm Weishaupt from the Appenzell, to the piece of fir wood he owned, where he made small wood log piles from trees that had just been chopped down. Images like these still came to me on my recent pilgrimage to Henry David Thoreau's "Walden" and the magic place of his wood cabin to walk around the tree-lined "Pond". Here I could smell the fragrances of my youth, James Fenimore Cooper's "Leather Stocking", and came to understand beyond time and space the growth of the plant world. Its soul.

In the still relatively short history of pictures in photography, which is full of outstanding evidence of just such moments, in the works of Ansel Adams it is not only me who encounters the deep experience of recognizing such feelings. Only through this message shared by everyone has it attained and maintained its extraordinary position. Only a few insiders were confident about the cool and sleek medium which through its tremendous empathy and its ability to quasi stop time and conjure up design became an incunabula. When I was able to marvel at the Californian Redwoods, I saw them through the eyes of Ansel Adams. My thanks go to him, the "trapper" of photographic history.

He is the measure for all his disciples and thanks to the gift of his pictures each beginner must find his own measure. When looking at the great number of photographs Heinrich Gohl has collected and put together for this publication and the exhibition of the same title, one can feel the long and intensive photographic heritage he has. Nothing can replace the direct "approach", the passage leading to the model, the journey, the adventure pared with knowledge, and the passion. The subject picture is always overpowering and more often than not cannot be let alone. Daubigny and Théodore Rousseau, the towering Courbet and the eternal Cézanne, greetings from all of them. Bonjour, new endangered world including Max Ernst the wise. The spell of the irretrievable surrounds them, the swan song before the suspected destruction – photography as an epitaph. Pictures as incantations/formulas. The fact that Heinrich Gohl himself so impressively found primordial landscapes and preserved them for us makes him the most qualified advocate of an endeavor that preserves the breath of the world.

Who could have imagined that photography would contribute to this wonder? The paper that the photography owes to the forest and its great many trees does not smell of silver oxide, but of the dew of a tender spruce sprout.
                                                    Guido Magnaguagno

DER WALD IN GESCHICHTE(N) UND GEGENWART

Wer hat dich, du schöner Wald,
Aufgebaut so hoch da droben?
Wohl den Meister will ich loben,
So lang noch mein' Stimm' erschallt.

Joseph von Eichendorff
«Der Jäger Abschied», 1810

Der Schriftsteller Robert Walser erinnerte sich 1913 in seinem Text «Der Wald» an einen Lehrer: «… der sagte uns, dass in verhältnismässig sehr kurzer Zeit das mittlere Europa ein einziger grosser Wald wäre, wenn die Zivilisation zurückginge. Wenn nicht Menschen da wären, die gegen das Wachsen des Waldes ankämpften, träte der Wald frei, als herrschendes Ganzes auf. Das gab uns zu denken.» Damit es nicht soweit komme, haben einige Nationen Gesetze erlassen, z.B. die Schweizerische Eidgenossenschaft das 1993 in Kraft getretene Waldgesetz, das im Artikel 3 bestimmt, dass die bestehende Waldfläche nicht vergrössert und nicht vermindert werden soll. Die USA haben während Bill Clintons Präsidialjahren die Unantastbarkeit der bestehenden Wälder in den amerikanischen Nationalparks gesetzlich garantiert.

Was Europa betrifft, so war der Sturm «Lothar» vom 26. und 27. Dezember 1999 seit Langem das verheerendste Ereignis für die Wälder Frankreichs, Deutschlands, Dänemarks; in den am stärksten betroffenen Kantonen der Schweiz betrug die Einbusse für die Waldbewirtschaftung mehr als drei Jahreserträge. Ihm war im Jahr 1990 der Sturm «Vivian» mit enormem Waldschaden vorangegangen. Es sind also auch die Kräfte der Natur, welche die von Robert Walsers Lehrer vorausgesehene Überwaldung Europas in Schranken halten. Anderseits aber beobachten wir, wie im Jahrzehnt nach den Katastrophen Bäume neu heranwachsen und das Unterholz unterdessen nur zu üppig sich erholt und verbreitet hat.

Doch knüpfen wir unseren weiteren Text nun doch wieder an Robert Walsers Befürchtungen ob der überhandnehmenden Waldflächen an, denn noch bis ins 19. Jahrhundert war Wald etwas Unheimliches – um es mild zu sagen. In den von den Brüdern Grimm gesammelten und 1819 veröffentlichten Volksmärchen ist Wald das Gebiet der Ausgegrenzten, so in «Schneewittchen», in «Hänsel und Gretel» und in «Rotkäppchen». Der historisch namhafte und in geringerem Umfang noch heute existierende Wald im Spessart war so legendär und gefürchtet, dass er in Wilhelm Hauffs Räubergeschichten mit dem Obertitel «Das Wirtshaus im Spessart» (1828) den Ort der Handlungen abgibt; damals und noch lange Zeit danach war er wirklich Zuflucht und Aktionsraum der Besitzlosen und Ausgestossenen, die sich zu Raub- und Mordbanden zusammenschlossen. Übrigens: Auch in Goethes Bühnenstück «Götz von Berlichingen» (1773) sowie in Schillers Schauspiel «Die Räuber» (1781) sind der Spessart oder die böhmischen Wälder Orte der dramatischen Handlungen.

In der Weltliteratur finden sich aber auch ungezählte Schilderungen der Verzauberungen im Wald. Zahlreich liest man sie etwa in Iwan Turgenjews «Aufzeichnungen eines Jägers» (1852), woraus hier nur eine Stelle angeführt sei:

«Die Sonne ist untergegangen, aber im Wald ist es noch hell. Die Luft ist rein und durchsichtig. Die Vögel zwitschern langhin, als ob sie sich miteinander besprächen. Das junge Gras glänzt mit dem Schimmer des Smaragds.

Mammutbäume
Kalifornien/USA, Juli 1997

Sequoias
California/USA, July 1997

Erlenbruch
Bonfol/Schweiz, Mai 1987

Alders
Bonfol/Switzerland, May 1987

Man wartet geduldig. Im Waldesinnern wird es dunkel. Das hellrote Licht der Abendröte gleitet über die Wurzeln und Äste der Bäume hin, erhebt sich höher und immer höher, geht über von den unteren, fast nackten Ästen, zu den unbeweglichen, schlummernden Wipfeln … Und nun sind auch die höchsten Spitzen dunkel geworden. Der hochrote Himmel nimmt eine bläuliche Färbung an. Der Duft des Waldes macht sich stärker bemerkbar. Ein warmer, feuchter Lufthauch, der sich erhoben hat, erstirbt in der Nähe. Die Vögel entschlummern, doch nicht alle zugleich, sondern je nach den Arten: Jetzt sind die Buchfinken verstummt, nach einigen Augenblicken werden auch die Grasmücken still, und nach ihnen die Goldammern. Im Wald wird es dunkler und immer dunkler. Die Bäume verschmelzen zu wuchtigen schwarzen Gebilden. Am blauen Himmel treten schüchtern die ersten Sternchen hervor. Alle Vögel schlafen. Einzig die Gartenrotschwänzchen und die kleinen Spechte lassen noch hin und wieder einen schläfrigen Ruf erschallen … Aber nun sind auch sie still geworden.»[1]

Wer hört beim Lesen dieser Zeilen nicht die Klänge von Richard Wagners «Siegfriedidyll» (1870)?

Und wer sieht nicht mit dem «inneren Auge» die in der gleichen Epoche gemalten Wald-Bilder einerseits der russischen Schule (z.B. von Iwan Iwanowitsch Schischkin), andrerseits diejenigen der französischen Vor-Im-

[1] Aus «Jermolaj und die Müllerin». Aus dem Russischen übertragen von Dora Berndl Friedmann. Zürich, Manesse, 1974, S. 45 f.

pressionisten? Wir denken an jene Maler, die sich in der Ortschaft Barbizon (bei Fontainebleau) niedergelassen haben, um fern von dem städtischen Paris (und der meist unverständigen «Salon»-Jurierung) im nahen Wald die Motive für ihre Gemälde zu finden und die in der Kunstgeschichte als «École de Barbizon» bekannt geworden sind: Théodore Rousseau, Henri Harpignies, Narcisse Diaz de la Peña und neben manchen anderen auch der junge Claude Monet. In der gleichen Epoche (vor 1880) waren in den Vereinigten Staaten die Künstler der «Hudson River School» (mit Thomas Cole, Albert Bierstadt und Frederic Church) am Werk, um in sowohl riesengrossen als auch grandiosen Gemälden die Waldgebiete Nordamerikas zu schildern. Ihnen waren mit Schilderungen der amerikanischen Wälder die Schriftsteller James Fenimore Cooper (The Last of the Mohicans, mit der Figur des «Leatherstocking» = «Lederstrumpf», 1826) sowie Henry Thoreau (etwa mit dem Buch «Walden», 1854) vorausgegangen.

In der französischen Literatur hat René de Chateaubriand seine im Jahrzehnt der Französischen Revolution unternommenen Fusswanderungen durch die amerikanischen Wälder beschrieben (Attala, 1801; René, 1802), aber die zitierenswerteste Stelle über die Wälder Nordamerikas findet sich in Alexis de Toquevilles «De la démocratie en Amérique» von 1835; ich übersetze:

«…Die Wälder breiteten dunkle und melancholische Decken über die Flüsse. Man sah dort kaum andere Bäume als die Fichte, die Lärche, die grüne Eiche, den wilden Olivenbaum und den Lorbeer. Wenn man jedoch diesen ersten Baumgürtel durchquert hatte, trat man in das Dunkel des Urwalds ein; hier fanden sich untereinander die allergrössten Bäume, welche auf beiden Erdhälften wachsen. Die Platane, die Katalpa (Trompetenbaum), der Zuckerahorn und die Virginia-Pappel kreuzten ihre Äste mit jenen der Eiche, der Buche und der Linde.

Wie in den von den Menschen bewirtschafteten Wäldern schlug der Tod hier ohne Unterlass zu, doch war niemand da, um die abgebrochenen und abgestorbenen Äste wegzuräumen. So schichteten sich denn die einen über die andern, bevor die Zeit sie recht schnell in Staub verfallen liess und Platz für Neues schuf. Und so, inmitten der Trümmer, vollzog sich unablässig die Arbeit des Neubeginns. Kletterpflanzen und Gräser aller Arten brachen sich Bahn durch die Trümmer hindurch; sie krochen den umgestürzten Stämmen entlang, nisteten sich in dem Mehlstaub ein, hoben und durchbrachen die brüchige Rinde, welche sie noch bedeckten, und öffneten den jungen Schösslingen neue Wege. So half der Tod sozusagen dem Weiterleben. Das eine wie das andere war gegenwärtig, als wollten beide ihr Werk zusammenlegen und vermischen.»

Von den Wäldern, die noch am Anfang und in der Mitte des 19. Jahrhunderts Nordmerika bedeckten, die Maler begeisterten und die Schriftsteller inspirierten, sind nicht viele übrig geblieben. Aufs Höchste intensivierte Landwirtschaft, Verstädterung, Shopping-Centers und manche andere Errungenschaften des kommerziellen Bestrebens haben sie verschwinden lassen und wohl auch zu Unwettern beigetragen. Allerdings: Die durch den «National Park Service Act» vom Jahr 1916 geschützten Waldzonen in fast jedem Bundesstaat der USA haben sie doch zu einem Bestandteil des amerikanischen Patrimoniums werden lassen.

Umso grösser ist die Bedeutung, welche die fotografischen Dokumente aus den amerikanischen Nationalparks etwa des grossen Kamera-Künstlers Ansel Adams (1902–1984) erlangt haben. Andere in dieser Ausstellung und in diesem Buch auftretende Fotografen arbeiten in seinem Sinn weiter, wobei man sehr oft von «Bildnissen», von Baum-Porträts sprechen kann.

Doch zurück zu Europa. Die Furcht des Schülers Robert Walser, dass seine Heimat von Wald überdeckt würde, ist heute, war seinerzeit und ist schon immer unbegründet gewesen – dafür haben die Menschen von jeher gesorgt. Denn sie bedurften und bedürfen der Bäume aus den Wäldern um des Holzes willen – nicht im kleinen Massstab für Feuer und Werkzeug, sondern in grossem, in riesigem Ausmass für Schiffbau und Waffenarsenal. Viele Mittelmeerlandschaften zeigen noch heute baumlose Hügel, entwaldete Berge und kahle Gebirge, die von den antiken Kriegsmächten – vor allem im römischen Imperium – der Wälder beraubt worden sind. Doch nicht anders haben im Norden die Wikinger weite Zonen von Island um

Fichtenwald
Alaska/USA, Oktober 1985

Spruce forest
Alaska/USA, October 1985

24

Stieleiche
Bubendorf/Schweiz, Februar 1988

Pedunculate Oak
Bubendorf/Switzerland, February 1988

des Schiffbaus willen kahl geschlagen. Und ebenso die Kriegsheere in England und in Schottland.

In Shakespeares Drama «Macbeth» (1603) wird dem mörderischen Titelhelden mehrmals versichert, er habe in seiner Festung Dunsinane nichts zu fürchten bis zum Zeitpunkt, «until Birnam Wood come to Dunsinane Hill» (IV. Akt, 1. Szene; V. Akt, 3., 4. und 5. Szenen) – also bis der Wald von Birnam sich auf sein Schloss zubewege und vor seiner Festung stünde. Und das geschieht nun in der Tat als Schluss des Dramas: Der Wald von Birnam steht vor Macbeths Festung und der Titelheld wird im Schwerter-Zweikampf überwältigt und getötet. Ists der Wald, sinds die Bäume von Birnam? Nein: es sind die Pfeile und die Bogen, die aus dem Kahlschlag des Waldes von Birnam gefertigt worden sind. (Apropos: Welch besseres warnendes Gleichnis liesse sich nicht heute in Bezug auf den Raubbau, z.B. im Amazonas-Gebiet, anführen? Wir kommen darauf zurück.)

So weit so gut – es waren Rückblicke auf Vergangenes. Wie stehts gegenwärtig weltweit mit den Wäldern?

Alarmierend ist der Raubbau in den grossen Waldflächen unserer Erde in mehreren Ländern von Südamerika – besonders in Brasiliens Amazonas-Urwald, in Indonesien, wo in den vergangenen 50 Jahren vierzig Prozent der Urwälder zerstört worden sind, sowie in Sibirien und in Myanmar (bis 1989 «Burma» genannt). Die grossflächigen und zumeist ungesetzlichen Rodungen geschehen einerseits um des Marktwerts des Holzes willen, ander-

seits, um Weidland für Rinderzucht (für die Fleischeinlage in den «hamburgers») zu gewinnen. Ganz aktuell sind die Waldbrände in Borneo und Malaysia, die um des Anbaus von Palmen willen zur Gewinnung von Bio-Kraftstoff aus dem Palmöl (statt Benzin aus Erdöl) gerodet werden; insgesamt werden gegenwärtig (Ende 2006) auf 600 000 Hektar Ölpalmen angepflanzt, denen eine entsprechend grosse Waldfläche zum Opfer gefallen ist[2].

Weltweit aber hat die Entwaldung in den jüngst vergangenen Jahren abgenommen, namentlich in El Salvador und in der Dominikanischen Republik. In Russland und Skandinavien, in China und Indien, in Südkorea und Vietnam nehmen die Waldflächen gegenwärtig zu[3].

Im Brennpunkt des Waldalarms und Wälderschutzes steht das Amazonasgebiet Brasiliens. Unsere Quelle für die nachstehenden Bemerkungen ist unter anderen die Internet-Adresse «AMAZONAS.de», deren mannigfalte Inhalte und Verweise wie sonst nichts anderes zu unserem Thema gehören.

Die Veränderungen im Amazonas-Regenwald sind offensichtlich. Bis zum Jahr 2000 sind etwa 14 Prozent der Waldflächen zerstört worden; zum Zeitpunkt der Drucklegung dieser Zeilen sind es viel mehr. Zunehmend dominieren schnell wachsende, grosse Bäume das Ökosystem, während bei den kleineren Bäumen von einem Massensterben gesprochen wird, was auf die Treibhaus-

[2] The Wall Street Journal, 5. und 15. Dezember 2006
[3] The Economist, 18. November 2006

25

Valle Bavona
Tessin/Schweiz, Oktober 1995

Valle Bavona
Ticino/Switzerland, October 1995

gase zurückzuführen sei. Weitere mögliche Ursachen für die Zerstörung des Ökosystems im Amazonas-Regenwald sind veränderte Temperaturen, vermehrte Sonneneinstrahlung sowie unterschiedliche Regenmengen. Vor allem aber vernichten Strassenbau und flächendeckender Kahlschlag zur räuberischen Holzgewinnung den Amazonaswald unwiederbringlich. Anschliessend schwemmt der Regen die Humusschicht fort. Die gegenwärtig weltweit vor sich gehenden Abholzungen beeinflussen – so lautet die gegenwärtige Prognose – das Klima auf der ganzen Erdkugel. Gemäss der Organisation Global Forest Watch werden in zwanzig Jahren vierzig Prozent der Wälder auf der Erde nicht mehr vorhanden sein. So ist denn auch die vom Basler Kunsthändler und Museumsgründer im Jahr 200X errichtete Stiftung «Art for Tropical Forests» zwar in der Lage, mit Geldzuwendungen die Rodungen im Amazonaswald einzuschränken, aber bei Weitem nicht zu verhindern.

Nun verbinden sich mit dem Wort «Amazonas» natürlich nicht nur Gedanken an Raubbau und Protest, vielmehr waren (und sind noch?) die riesigen Waldgebiete entlang des Orinoko- und des Amazonasstroms Wohnstätte von Indianer-Völkern und Traumziele von Weltenbummlern. Die Tourismusindustrie hat verlockende und wahrscheinlich das Überleben garantierende Reiserouten und Unterkünfte bereitgestellt, die noch immer ein tiefes Wald-, ein sich unvergessbar einprägendes (Ur-)Walderlebnis möglich machen (Marajò Park Resort, Amazon Village und Ama-

zon Ecopark Lodge heissen drei der zahlreichen angebotenen Destinationen). Vor allem das Nächtigen im Freien lässt den Wald als tausendstimmiges, nie verstummendes Orchester sowie als licht- und glimmervolles Naturspektakel erfahren – und auch als erbarmungslose Mückenplage. Man erinnert sich an das Leiden an Mückenstichen des Pioniers der Amazonas-Erkundung, nämlich des Forschungsreisenden Alexander von Humboldt (1769–1859), der zwischen 1799 und 1804 das nördliche Südamerika mit vielen Apparaten und Trägern bereiste und seine Beobachtungen in gelehrten Schriften sowie in den Erinnerungsbüchern «Ansichten der Natur» (1807) und «Auf Steppen und Strömen Südamerikas» (zuerst französisch, 1859–1860) festgehalten hat. Darin lesen wir unter anderem: «Der Wald, der den steilen Abhang des Berges bedeckt, ist einer der dichtesten, den ich je gesehen habe. Die Bäume sind wirklich ungeheuer hoch und dick. Unter ihrem dichten, dunkelgrünen Laub herrscht ständig ein Dämmerlicht, ein Dunkel, weit tiefer als in unseren Tannen-, Eichen- und Buchenwäldern. Zu den aromatischen Gerüchen, welche Blüten, Früchte, sogar das Holz verbreiten, kommt ein anderer, wie man ihn bei uns im Herbst bei nebligem Wetter riecht.» Humboldts tiefes Walderlebnis umfasste Fauna und Flora, aber seine Berichte schildern – abgesehen von der Mückenplage – auch einzelne gigantische Bäume. «An die Stelle der europäischen Buchen und Ahorne treten hier die grossartigen Gestalten der Ceiba-Bäume, der Praga- und Irasse-

Palmen. Unzählige Quellen brechen aus den Bergwänden. Die Feuchtigkeit, die sie verbreiten, fördert das Wachstum der grossen Bäume…»

So war es einmal…

Über den Ceiba-Baum (enterolobium pentandra), den heiligen Baum der Maya, hat ein Reisender unserer Tage geschrieben: «… die eindrucksvollsten Bäume sind die Ceiba-Bäume. Sie sind die Weltenbäume der Maya. In Regionen mit mehr Grundwasser, wo die Vegetation dichter ist, müssen diese Bäume entsprechend höher geworden sein, mit einem Stamm so lang wie der Durchmesser der Krone. Doch leider habe ich keine mehr gesehen, selbst in Regionen, in denen gemäss Fotografien vor nicht allzu langer Zeit noch vereinzelt solche Riesen standen.» Dieser Bericht eines zeitgenössischen Reisenden klingt wie ein Requiem für einen Baum und steht hier als Memento mori für den Wald.

Reinhold Hohl

Silberweide
Büren/Schweiz, Oktober 1996

White Willow
Büren/Switzerland, October 1996

THE FOREST IN HISTORY (STORIES) AND PRESENT

In 1913, the writer Robert Walser recalled in his text "Der Wald" (The Forest) of a teacher of him who: "… told us that in a relatively short time the middle of Europe would be one single big forest, provided civilisation would recede. If humans weren't here to fight against its growth, the forest would become free to rule as a whole. This made us think."

So as not to get this far, some nations passed laws, for instance the Swiss Confederacy the "Waldgesetz" (Forest Law) which decrees in article 3 that the existing forest area may not be enlarged nor reduced. Under Bill Clinton's presidency, a United States bylaw guaranteed the inviolability of the existing forests in the American national parks. As concerns Europe, the storm "Lothar" of December 26 and 27, 1999, was the most devastating occurrence for the forests of France, Germany and Denmark for a long time. In the most affected cantons in Switzerland the loss encountered in forest cultivation amounted to that of an annual yield of three years. In 1990, the storm "Vivian" had already left enormous damage to the forests. The forces of nature that were predicted by Robert Walser's teacher are the ones that keep the overgrowth of the forests in their place. On the other hand, we can observe, how one decade after these disasters trees have regrown and the underbrush had profusely recovered and spread.

Still, let us remember in this text that Robert Walser's apprehensions about the size of the wooded areas getting out of hand were not unfounded, because up until the 19th century forests were perceived as being something eerie – to put it mildly. In the collected and in 1819 published folk tales the woods was an area for the segregated like in "Snow White", "Hansel and Gretel" and "Little Red Riding Hood". The historically famous and to a lesser degree still existing forest in the Spessart, was a legendary and dreaded place as depicted in Wilhelm Hauff's tale of robbers "Das Wirtshaus im Spessart" (The Tavern in Spessart) (1828); back then and for a long time after it was really a refuge for the poor and outcasts who ganged together to rob and murder anyone who may have been passing through. Incidentally, in Goethe's "Götz von Berlichingen" (Goetz of Berlichingen) (1773), as well as Schiller's "Die Räuber" (The Robbers) (1781), the Spessart and the Bohemian woods are scenes of dramatic acts. The world literature contains but innumerable narrations of enchantments in the forest. For example, one can read of them in Iwan Turgenjews numerous "Recordings of a Hunter" (1852), of which to mention only one here:

"The sun has gone down, but it is still bright in the forest. The air is clean and clear. The birds are still singing as if they were conversing with one another. The young grass shines with the lustre of the emerald. One waits patiently. It is getting dark within the forest. The bright red of the afterglow glides over the roots and

Kokospalmen, Everglades
Florida/USA, August 1983

Coco Palms, Everglades
Florida/USA, August 1983

Grannenkiefern, White Mountains
Kalifornien/USA, August 1998

Bristlecone Pines, White Mountains
California/USA, August 1998

branches of the trees, ever rising, goes from the lower, almost naked branches, to the steadfast, slumbering tree tops … And now the highest peaks have turned dark as well. The bright red sky gradually takes on a bluish hue. The scent of the forest is becoming stronger. A warm, moist breath of air that arose fades away nearby. The birds doze off, not all of them at once, but each according to its breed: Now the chaffinch falls silent, after a few moments the midges will be still, the yellowhammers after that. The forest turns darker and darker. The trees melt into bulky black shapes. The first little stars appear timidly on the dark blue sky. All birds are now asleep. Only the garden redstarts and the small woodpeckers sound their sleepy call once in a while … But now they have become still as well."[1]

By reading these lines, who will not hear the sounds of Richard Wagner's "Siegfriedidyll" (Siegfried's Serenity) (1870)?

And who cannot see with the "inner eye" the painted forest pictures of the same epoch, on the one side of the Russian school (i.e. by Iwan Iwanowitsch Schischkin), and on the other those by the French pre-impressionists? We are thinking of those painters who settled in the community of Barbizon (near Fontainebleau), to get away from the urban Paris (and the mostly in-

comprehensible "drawing room" jury system), to find in the near woods motives for their paintings that became known in art history as "École de Barbizon" (the Barbizon School): Théodore Rousseau, Henri Harpignies, Narcisse Diaz de la Peña and next to many others also the young Claude Monet. During the same epoch (before 1880), in the United States the artists of the "Hudson River School" (with Thomas Cole, Albert Bierstadt and Frederic Church) were at work portraying in giant as well as grandiose canvases the wooded areas of North America. Ahead of these, portrayals of the American forests were written by the author James Fenimore Cooper (The Last of the Mohicans, with the character "Leatherstocking", 1826) as well as Henry Thoreau (for example with the book "Walden", 1854).

In the French literature, René de Chateaubriand described his wanderings through the American forests during the decade of the French revolution (Attala, 1801; René, 1802), but the most worthy place of citation about the forests of North America can be found in Alexis de Toqueville's "De la démocratie en Amérique" of 1835; I'm translating:

"… The woods spread dark and melancholy covers over the rivers. One could hardly see trees other than the spruce, the tamarack, the green oak tree, the wild olive tree and the laurel. However, once one has walked through this first belt of trees, one stepped into the

[1] From "Jermolaj und die Müllerin". From the Russian by Dora Berndl Friedmann. Zürich, Manesse, 1974, p. 45 f.

dark of the primeval forest; here the biggest of all trees that grow on both halves of the earth have found each other. The sycamore, the catalpa (also Indian bean), the sugar maple and the Virginia poplar cross their branches with those of the oak, the beech and the linden.

Like in the woods cultivated by man death here strikes incessantly, still nobody was here to clear the broken and dead branches. Thus, they layered one over the other, before time quickly let them rot into dust to make room for a change to something new. Accordingly, in the midst of this wreckage the work for a new beginning ceaselessly took place. Twiners and grasses of all kinds were blazing their trails through the wreckage; they were creeping along the toppled trees to nest in the mealy dust, lifted and broke through the brittle rind, which they still covered to open new ways for the young sapling. In a way death helped life to continue. Equally, the one as well as the other was present, as if both would want to combine and mix their work."

Not many of the forests are left that still covered the states of America during the middle of the 19th century and that elated painters and inspired writers. Farming intensified to ultimate perfection, urbanisation, shopping centers and many other achievements of the commercial industry made them disappear and may have well contributed to the natural disasters of today. Admittedly, the "National Park Service Act" of 1916 pro-

tected wood areas in almost every state of the Union and allowed them to become an integral part of the American patrimony.

The more so is the importance that the photographic documents of the American national parks, for example from the great camera artist Ansel Adams (1902–1984), have attained. Others in this exhibition and photographers appearing in this book continue to work in his spirit, whereby one can often speak about "effigies" of tree portraits.

But back to Europe. The fear of the pupil Robert Walser that his homeland would be covered by woods is still today as it was then unfounded; humans have always taken care of this. Because they were always and are still in want of the trees from the forests for the sake of lumber – not for small measures for fire and tools, but to a large extend for ships and armour. Many of the Mediterranean landscapes still show treeless hillsides, deforested bare mountains that were robbed of the woods by the antique war powers – especially during Roman imperialism. The Vikings in the north were not much different since they cut clear wide zones of Iceland to build ships. Likewise did the armies of England and Scotland.

In Shakespeare's drama "Macbeth" (1603), the murderous protagonist is repeatedly reassured that he must not be afraid in his fortress Dunsinane up until the time, "until Birnam Wood come to Dunsinane Hill"

Akazie vor Kilimandscharo
Ostafrika, Dezember 1964

Acazia, Kilimandscharo
East Africa, December 1964

Ngorongoro Krater
Tansania/Afrika, Dezember 1964

Ngorongoro Crater
Tansania/Africa, December 1964

(4th act, 1st scene; 5th act, scenes 3, 4 and 5) – thus, until the wood of Birnam moves towards his castle to stand in front of the ramparts. This in fact happens at the end of the drama: The wood of Birnam is standing in front of Macbeth's fortress and the protagonist is overpowered and put to death. Is it the wood or the trees of Birnam? No: it is the arrows and the bows that were crafted from the cut down wood of Birnam. (Speaking of cutting down forests: No better cautionary parable could be mentioned here with regard to the exploitation for instance of the Amazon? We shall return to this.) So far so good – a historical retrospect. But what about the current situation of the forests worldwide?

It is alarming to hear about the exploitation of large wooded areas on our planet in numerous countries in South America – especially the rain forest of the Amazon in Brazil –, in Indonesia, where in the last 50 years 40 percent of virgin forest was destroyed and what about the forests in Siberia and Myanmar (until 1989 called "Burma")? The mostly illegal uprooting of large areas happens because of the market value of wood, but, on the other hand, also to gain grounds for cattle breeding (for meat in "hamburgers"). Highly current are the forest fires raised in Borneo and Malaysia for the sake of palm cultivations for the production of bio-fuel from palm oil (instead of gasoline from crude oil). Currently, a total of 600,000 metric hectares (end of 2006) of oil palms are planted, having fallen pray to a corresponding wood area[2].

On a worldwide level, the forest clearance has receded in the most recent years, namely in El Salvador and in the Dominican Republic. In Russia and Scandinavia, in China and India, in South Korea and Vietnam, the wooded areas are currently increasing[3].

The Amazon region of Brazil is the focal point of this alarming situation and of the protection of forests. Our source for the following comments is among others the internet address "AMAZONAS.de", the various contents and references therein fit perfectly to our topic.

The changes in the Amazon rain forest are obvious. By the year 2000, approximately 14 percent of the forested area was destroyed; at the time of printing these lines this could well be much more. The rapidly growing large trees are dominating the ecological system at an accelerating pace, while there is talk about mass extinction of smaller trees that may be traced back to green house gases. Further possible causes of the destruction of the eco system of the Amazon rain forest are the changed temperatures, increased exposure to direct sunlight as well as varying precipitation. However, most of all, road construction and clearing of wide areas for predacious logging are irretrievably killing the Amazonian forest. Afterwards, the rain wears

[2] The Wall Street Journal, December 5 and 15, 2006.
[3] The Economist, November 18, 2006

Fichten
Gasterntal/Schweiz, September 1999

Spruces
Gasterntal/Switzerland, Septemper 1999

away the fragile topsoil. The current logging taking place worldwide will have – according to current forecast – a grave influence on the climate on our entire planet. According to the Organisation Global Forest, in twenty years, forty percent of the forests will no longer exist. The fund "Art for Tropical Forests" established in 2002 by the Basel art dealer and founder of the museum, may be able to curtail clear cutting in the Amazon forest with financial allowances, but by no means can it prevent it.

Now then, not only do we associate the word "Amazon" with thoughts about exploitation of nature and protest, the more so with the wooded areas along the Orinoko and the Amazon rivers and the dwellings of Indian nations becoming dream destinations for globetrotters. The tourism industry offers tempting travel routes and accommodations that probably guarantees survival, which still makes possible an impressive and memorable primordial forest experience (Marajò Park Resort, Amazon Village and Amazon Ecopark Lodge are three of the many offered destinations). Most of all, camping in the open allows one to experience the forest as a myriad, an orchestra never falling silent as well as a nature spectacle full of glimmering light – and the merciless plague of mosquitos. One remembers the suffering pioneers of the Amazon explorations and their mosquito bites, namely of the expedition traveller Alexander von Humboldt (1769–1859), who between 1799 and 1804 travelled by foot through South America with porters carrying numerous apparatuses to record his observations in learned writings as well as books of remembrance "Ansichten der Natur" (Views of Nature) (1807) and "Auf Steppen und Strömen Südamerikas" (On the Steppes and Streams of South America) (first in French, 1859–1860). Among other texts, we read in them: "The forest, covering the steep slope of the hill is one of the densest I ever saw. The trees are really enormously high and thick. Underneath their densely packed dark green leaves there is constant crepuscular light, a darkness far deeper than in our fir, oak and beech woods. Added to the aromatic scents spread by blossoms, fruit and even wood, another one is added much like the one one can smell in the autumn foggy weather at home." Humboldt's profound forest experience encompassed fauna and flora, but his recordings tell – aside from the mosquito plague – about several gigantic trees. "In place of the European beech and maple, the grandiose figures of the Ceiba trees, the Praga and Irasse palms arise here. Innumerable springs and shoots are sprouting out of the hillsides. The humidity spread by them, fosters the growth of the large trees…".

This is the way it was…

About the Ceiba tree (Enterolobium pentandra), the holy tree of the Mayan, a traveller of today wrote: "… the most impressing trees are the Ceiba trees.

They are the "World Tree" of the Mayan. In regions with more artesian water, where the vegetation is denser, these trees must accordingly have grown taller, with a stem as long as the diameter of the crown. Regretfully, I did not get to see any any longer, even in regions in which, according to photographs, some must have stood as giants not too long ago."

This account by a contemporary traveller sounds like a requiem for a tree and stands here as a memento mori for the forest.

Reinhold Hohl

Stieleiche
Rügen/Deutschland, August 2001

Pedunculate Oak
Rügen/Germany, August 2001

Heinrich Gohl (1926)
Egegik Bay, Aleuten
Alaska/USA, August 1967

Heinrich Gohl (1926)
Egegik Bay, Aleutian
Alaska/USA, August 1967

Ulrich Ackermann (1947)
Brooks Range, Koness River
Alaska/USA, Oktober 1981

Ulrich Ackermann (1947)
Brooks Range, Koness River
Alaska/USA, October 1981

Heinrich Gohl (1926)
Susitna River, Alaska Range
Alaska/USA, November 1985

Heinrich Gohl (1926)
Susitna River, Alaska Range
Alaska/USA, November 1985

Heinrich Gohl (1926)
Hemlocktannen, Muldrow Gebirge
Alaska/USA, Oktober 1985

Heinrich Gohl (1926)
Hemlock, Muldrow Mountains
Alaska/USA, October 1985

42

Heinrich Gohl (1926)
Denali National Park
Alaska/USA, November 1985

Heinrich Gohl (1926)
Denali National Park
Alaska/USA, November 1985

Heinrich Gohl (1926)
Denali National Park
Alaska/USA, November 1985

Heinrich Gohl (1926)
Denali National Park
Alaska/USA, November 1985

Heinrich Gohl (1926)
Kwipak Bay
Alaska/USA, 1985

Heinrich Gohl (1926)
Kwipak Bay
Alaska/USA, 1985

Heinrich Gohl (1926)
Cinder Bay, Aleuten
Alaska/USA, August 1967

Heinrich Gohl (1926)
Cinder Bay, Aleutian
Alaska/USA, August 1967

Heinrich Gohl (1926)
West Fork
Alaska/USA, Oktober 1985

Heinrich Gohl (1926)
West Fork
Alaska/USA, October 1985

47

Norbert Rosing (1953)
Sour Creek Mäander, Yellowstone NP
Wyoming/USA, Juli 1997

Norbert Rosing (1953)
Sour Creek Meander, Yellowstone NP
Wyoming/USA, July 1997

Heinrich Gohl (1926)
Nenana River
Alaska/USA, Juni 1967

Heinrich Gohl (1926)
Nenana River
Alaska/USA, June 1967

Norbert Rosing (1953)
Dampfende Mäander am Morgen, Yellowstone NP
Wyoming/USA, August 1997

Norbert Rosing (1953)
Meanders steaming in morning air, Yellowstone NP
Wyoming/USA, August 1997

Norbert Rosing (1953)
Hayden Valley
Wyoming/USA, September 1997

Norbert Rosing (1953)
Hayden Valley
Wyoming/USA, September 1997

52

Hans Strand (1955)
Kiefernwald, Fårö-Insel
Gotland/Schweden, Juli 1994

Hans Strand (1955)
Pine forest, Fårö Island
Gotland/Sweden, July 1994

Hans Strand (1955)
Alte Kiefern, Stora Sjöfallet NP
Lappland/Schweden, September 1994

Hans Strand (1955)
Old growth pine forest, Stora Sjöfallet NP
Lapland/Sweden, September 1994

Jan Töve (1958)
Windgeformter Kiefer
Saltö-Insel/Schweden, August 2002

Jan Töve (1958)
Windswept coastal pine forest
Saltö Island/Sweden, August 2002

Norbert Rosing (1953)
Bergfichtenwald, Brocken
Harz/Deutschland, Juni 1992

Norbert Rosing (1953)
Mountain spruce forest, Brocken
Harz/Germany, June 1992

Klaus Nigge (1956)
Steinbirkenwald
Süd-Kamtschatka/Russland, August 2003

Klaus Nigge (1956)
Stone birch forest
South-Kamtschatka/Russia, August 2003

Klaus Nigge (1956)
Bruchwald, Bialowieza NP
Polen, Februar 2003

Klaus Nigge (1956)
Cracked wood, Bialowieza NP
Poland, February 2003

Klaus Nigge (1956)
Flachland-Urwald, Bialowieza NP
Polen, Juli 2002

Klaus Nigge (1956)
Lowland primeval forest, Bialowieza NP
Poland, July 2002

Patrick Loertscher (1964)
Südbuchenwald, Te Urewra NP
Neuseeland, November 1999

Patrick Loertscher (1964)
Southern beech grove, Te Urewra NP
New Zealand, November 1999

Mike Hill (1949)
Wistmann's Wood, Dartmoor
Devon/England, Oktober 2000

Mike Hill (1949)
Wistmann's Wood, Dartmoor
Devon/UK, October 2000

Heinrich Gohl (1926)
Gemässigter Regenwald, Olympic NP
Washington/USA, Juni 1972

Heinrich Gohl (1926)
Hoh rain forest, Olympic NP
Washington/USA, June 1972

Cornelia Dörr (1963)
Araukarienwald, Villarica NP
Chile, Juni 2002

Cornelia Dörr (1963)
Araucaria forest, Parque National Villarica
Chile, June 2002

Heinrich Gohl (1926)
White Mountains
Arizona/USA, August 1977

Heinrich Gohl (1926)
White Mountains
Arizona/USA, August 1977

Heinrich Gohl (1926)
Bryce Canyon NP
Utah/USA, Oktober 1967

Heinrich Gohl (1926)
Bryce Canyon NP
Utah/USA, October 1967

Heinrich Gohl (1926)
Manos Valley
Colorado/USA, August 1972

Heinrich Gohl (1926)
Manos Valley
Colorado/USA, August 1972

Heinrich Gohl (1926)
Point Lobos
Kalifornien/USA, August 1997

Heinrich Gohl (1926)
Point Lobos
California/USA, August 1997

Heinrich Gohl (1926)
Pazifik-Küste
Kalifornien/USA, Juli 1997

Heinrich Gohl (1926)
Pacific Coast
California/USA, July 1997

Heinrich Gohl (1926)
Josuabäume, Yoshua Tree Wilderness
Kalifornien/USA, Juli 1997

Heinrich Gohl (1926)
Josua Trees, Yoshua Tree Wilderness
California/USA, July 1997

Heinrich Gohl (1926)
Gemässigter Regenwald, Olympic NP
Washington/USA, April 1981

Heinrich Gohl (1926)
Hoh rain forest, Olympic NP
Washington/USA, April 1981

Heinrich Gohl (1926)
Küstenmammutbäume, Sequoia NP
Kalifornien/USA, Juli 1997

Heinrich Gohl (1926)
Sequoias, Sequoia NP
California/USA, July 1997

Heinrich Gohl (1926)
Douglasien, Olympic NP
Washington/USA, August 1998

Heinrich Gohl (1926)
Douglas-firs, Olympic NP
Washington/USA, August 1998

Heinrich Gohl (1926)
Küstenmammutbäume, Sequoia NP
Kalifornien/USA, August 1997

Heinrich Gohl (1926)
Sequoias, Sequoia NP
California/USA, August 1997

Ansel Adams (1902–1984)
Jeffrey-Kiefer, Sentinel Dome, Yosemite NP
Kalifornien/USA, 1940

Ansel Adams (1902–1984)
Jeffrey Pine, Sentinel Dome, Yosemite NP
California/USA, 1940

Ansel Adams (1902–1984)
Yosemite Valley im Winter, Yosemite NP
Kalifornien/USA, ca. 1940

Ansel Adams (1902–1984)
Yosemite Valley in winter, Yosemite NP
California/USA, approx. 1940

75

Edward Weston (1886–1958)
Louisiana
USA, 1941

Edward Weston (1886–1958)
Louisiana
USA, 1941

Edward Weston (1886–1958)
Juniper, Lake Tenaya
Kalifornien/USA, 1937

Edward Weston (1886–1958)
Juniper, Lake Tenaya
California/USA, 1937

Heinrich Gohl (1926)
Grannenkiefer–1, Inyo Forest
Kalifornien/USA, Juli 1997

Heinrich Gohl (1926)
Bristlecone pine–1, Inyo Forest
California/USA, July 1997

Heinrich Gohl (1926)
Grannenkiefern–2, Inyo Forest
Kalifornien/USA, Juni 1997

Heinrich Gohl (1926)
Bristlecone pines–2, Inyo Forest
California/USA, June 1997

80

Heinrich Gohl (1926)
Grannenkiefer–3, Inyo Forest
Kalifornien/USA, August 1998

Heinrich Gohl (1926)
Bristlecone pine–3, Inyo Forest
California/USA, August 1998

Heinrich Gohl (1926)
Grannenkiefern–4, Inyo Forest
Kalifornien/USA, August 1998

Heinrich Gohl (1926)
Bristlecone pines–4, Inyo Forest
California/USA, August 1998

Heinrich Gohl (1926)
Grannenkiefern–5, Inyo Forest
Kalifornien/USA, Juli 1998

Heinrich Gohl (1926)
Bristlecone pines–5, Inyo Forest
California/USA, July 1998

Heinrich Gohl (1926)
Grannenkiefern–6, Inyo Forest
Kalifornien/USA, August 1998

Heinrich Gohl (1926)
Bristlecone pines–6, Inyo Forest
California/USA, August 1998

83

Heinrich Gohl (1926)
Tres Plimas, White Mountains
Kalifornien/USA, August 1997

Heinrich Gohl (1926)
Tres Plimas, White Mountains
California/USA, August 1997

Christian Vogt (1946)
Mauna Loa, Big Island
Hawaii/USA, Februar 2005

Christian Vogt (1946)
Mauna Loa, Big Island
Hawaii/USA, February 2005

Christian Vogt (1946)
Olema Valley, Point Reyes
Kalifornien/USA, März 2005

Christian Vogt (1946)
Olema Valley, Point Reyes
California/USA, March 2005

Christian Vogt (1946)
Bois du Roi, Sommières
Frankreich, November 2003

Christian Vogt (1946)
Bois du Roi, Sommières
France, November 2003

Heinrich Gohl (1926)
Silberweide, Valle Maggia
Tessin/Schweiz, Oktober 2006

Heinrich Gohl (1926)
White Willow, Valle Maggia
Ticino/Switzerland, October 2006

Heinrich Gohl (1926)
Kastanien, Valle Bavona
Tessin/Schweiz, Oktober 2006

Heinrich Gohl (1926)
Chestnuts, Valle Bavona
Ticino/Switzerland, October 2006

Heinrich Gohl (1926)
Eremitage, Arlesheim
Schweiz, Sommer 2006

Heinrich Gohl (1926)
Eremitage, Arlesheim
Switzerland, Summer 2006

Heinrich Gohl (1926)
Birkenwald an der Peccia
Tessin/Schweiz, Juli 1998

Heinrich Gohl (1926)
Birches, Peccia River
Ticino/Switzerland, July 1998

Heinrich Gohl (1926)
Kastanien-Birkenwald
Tessin/Schweiz, November 1998

Heinrich Gohl (1926)
Chestnut-Birches
Ticino/Switzerland, November 1998

Heinrich Gohl (1926)
Kastanienwald, Fontana
Tessin/Schweiz, August 1994

Heinrich Gohl (1926)
Chestnuts, Fontana
Ticino/Switzerland, August 1994

94

Heinrich Gohl (1926)
Silberweide, Büren a. A.
Bern/Schweiz, Februar 1998

Heinrich Gohl (1926)
White Willow, Büren a. A.
Berne/Switzerland, February 1998

Heinrich Gohl (1926)
Alte Aare
Schweiz, April 1984

Heinrich Gohl (1926)
Old Aare
Switzerland, April 1984

Heinrich Gohl (1926)
Auenwald, Büren a. A.
Bern/Schweiz, Februar 1995

Heinrich Gohl (1926)
Lowland forest, Büren a. A.
Berne/Switzerland, February 1995

Heinrich Gohl (1926)
Auenwald, Seeland
Schweiz, Februar 1998

Heinrich Gohl (1926)
Lowland forest, Seeland
Switzerland, February 1998

Hans Strand (1955)
Kapur-Bäume
Selangor/Malaysia, März 1996

Hans Strand (1955)
Kapur trees
Selangor/Malaysia, March 1996

Ernst Haas (1921–1986)
In der Mitte des Waldes
1971

Ernst Haas (1921–1986)
In the Middle of the Woods
1971

Ernst Haas (1921–1986)
Fluss aus Gold
1971

Ernst Haas (1921–1986)
River of Gold
1971

Patrick Loertscher (1964)
Lärchenwald, Derborance
Wallis/Schweiz, Oktober 2003

Patrick Loertscher (1964)
Larch forest, Derborance
Valais/Switzerland, October 2003

Heinrich Gohl (1926)
Great Gulf Wilderness
New Hampshire/USA, Oktober 1979

Heinrich Gohl (1926)
Great Gulf Wilderness
New Hampshire/USA, October 1979

Hans-Peter Schaub (1961)
Kiefern, Pfälzerwald
Deutschland, Frühjahr 1999

Hans-Peter Schaub (1961)
Pines, Palatinate Woods
Germany, Spring 1999

Heinrich Gohl (1926)
Maine
USA, Oktober 1979

Heinrich Gohl (1926)
Maine
USA, October 1979

105

Albert Renger-Patzsch (1897–1966)
Fichtengruppe, Reichardswald
Nürnberg/Deutschland, 1958

Albert Renger-Patzsch (1897–1966)
Spruces, Reichardswald
Nuremberg/Germany, 1958

Albert Renger-Patzsch (1897–1966)
Silberweiden im Donau-Auenwald
Ingolstadt/Deutschland, 1958

Albert Renger-Patzsch (1897–1966)
White Willows, Donau lowland forest
Ingolstadt/Germany, 1958

107

Heinrich Gohl (1926)
Saba-Urwald
Reinhardshagen/Deutschland, Juli 2000

Heinrich Gohl (1926)
Saba primeval forest
Reinhardshagen/Germany, July 2000

Heinrich Gohl (1926)
Saba-Urwald
Reinhardshagen/Deutschland, Juli 2000

Heinrich Gohl (1926)
Saba primeval forest
Reinhardshagen/Germany, July 2000

Heinrich Gohl (1926)
Stieleiche
Wildenstein/Schweiz, Mai 1997

Heinrich Gohl (1926)
Pedunculate Oak
Wildenstein/Switzerland, May 1997

Heinrich Gohl (1926)
Traubeneiche, Insel Vilm
Rügen/Deutschland, Oktober 2000

Heinrich Gohl (1926)
Sessile Oak, Vilm Island
Rügen/Germany, October 2000

Cornelia Dörr (1963)
Pazifischer Regenwald, Olympic NP
Washington/USA, Juni 2002

Cornelia Dörr (1963)
Pacific rainforest, Olympic NP
Washington/USA, June 2002

Graeme Matthews (1949)
Araukarien, Vulkan Llaima
Chile, 1993

Graeme Matthews (1949)
Monky puzzle, Volcan Llaima
Chile, 1993

Hans Strand (1955)
Eukalyptus, Blue Mountains
New South Wales/Australien, März 1996

Hans Strand (1955)
Eucalyptus trees, Blue Mountains
New South Wales/Australia, March 1996

Günter Ziesler (1939)
Eukalyptuswald im Nebel, Wombargo Saddle, Alpine NP
Victoria/Australien, November 1999

Günter Ziesler (1939)
Eucalyptus forest in mist, Wombargo Saddle, Alpine NP
Victoria/Australia, November 1999

Hans Strand (1955)
Eukalyptus, Terra Bluga NP
Victoria/Australien, März 1996

Hans Strand (1955)
Blue gums, Terra Bluga NP
Victoria/Australia, March 1996

Urs Martin Bachmann (1961)
Waldlandschaft, Kawarau River
Süd-Neuseeland, Mai 1992

Urs Martin Bachmann (1961)
Forest landscape, Kawarau River
South New Zealand, Mai 1992

Günter Ziesler (1939)
Tropischer Regenwald nach Regenschauer, Gomantong Sabah
Borneo/Malaysia, Februar 1994

Günter Ziesler (1939)
Tropical rainforest after heavy rain, Gomantong Sabah
Borneo/Malaysia, February 1994

Günter Ziesler (1939)
Subtropischer Regenwald im Nebel, Dorrigo NP
New South Wales/Australien, Dezember 1999

Günter Ziesler (1939)
Subtropical rainforest in mist, Dorrigo NP
New South Wales/Australia, December 1999

Günter Ziesler (1939)
Segama-River, Danum Valley
Borneo/Malaysia, Februar 1994

Günter Ziesler (1939)
Segama-River, Danum Valley
Borneo/Malaysia, February 1994

Günter Ziesler (1939)
Bergwald, Cayambe-Coca-Reservat
Ecuador, 1977

Günter Ziesler (1939)
Mountain rainforest, Cayambe-Coca Reserve
Ecuador, 1977

Franz Lanting (1951)
Nebelwald
Costa Rica, 1998

Franz Lanting (1951)
Cloud forest
Costa Rica, 1998

Franz Lanting (1951)
Flussmäander, Rio Torre
Peru, 1993

Franz Lanting (1951)
Meandering river, Rio Torre
Peru, 1993

123

Konrad Wothe (1952)
Seitenarm des Kinabatangan River
Borneo/Malaysia, März 1994

Konrad Wothe (1952)
Anabranch of Kinabatangan River
Borneo/Malaysia, March 1994

Konrad Wothe (1952)
Regenwald, Danum Valley
Borneo/Malaysia, März 1993

Konrad Wothe (1952)
Rainforest, Danum Valley
Borneo/Malaysia, March 1993

Heinrich Gohl (1926)
Würgefeigen, Everglades
Florida/USA, März 1981

Heinrich Gohl (1926)
Wild banyantree, Everglades
Florida/USA, March 1981

Günter Ziesler (1939)
Tropischer Regenwald, Danum Valley
Borneo/Malaysia, März 1994

Günter Ziesler (1939)
Tropical rainforest, Danum Valley
Borneo/Malaysia, March 1994

Patrick Loertscher (1964)
Antarktischer Buchenwald, Lamington NP
Queensland/Australien, September 2002

Patrick Loertscher (1964)
Antarctic beech forest, Lamington NP
Queensland/Australia, September 2002

Günter Ziesler (1939)
Subtropischer Regenwald, Eungella NP
Queensland/Australien, Dezember 1999

Günter Ziesler (1939)
Subtropical rainforest, Eungella NP
Queensland/Australia, December 1999

Heinrich Gohl (1926)
Mangroven-Sumpf, Everglades
Florida/USA, März 1983

Heinrich Gohl (1926)
Mangrove swamp, Everglades
Florida/USA, March 1983

Heinrich Gohl (1926)
Sumpfwald, Mississippi-Delta
Mississippi/USA, August 1972

Heinrich Gohl (1926)
Big Swamp, Mississippi delta
Mississippi/USA, August 1972

Heinrich Gohl (1926)
Yucca-Dickicht, Everglades
Florida/USA, Februar 1986

Heinrich Gohl (1926)
Yuccas, Everglades
Florida/USA, February 1986

Heinrich Gohl (1926)
Sumpfschraubenbäume, Madeira Bay
Florida/USA, April 1981

Heinrich Gohl (1926)
Swampscrewpalms, Madeira Bay
Florida/USA, April 1981

Heinrich Gohl (1926)
Taylor Slough
Florida/USA, August 1977

Heinrich Gohl (1926)
Taylor Slough
Florida/USA, August 1977

Heinrich Gohl (1926)
Golf von Mexiko
USA, März 1981

Heinrich Gohl (1926)
Gulf of Mexico
USA, March 1981

135

Heinrich Gohl (1926)
Sumpfzypressen, Okefenokee-Sumpf
Georgia/USA, November 1967

Heinrich Gohl (1926)
Pond Cypress, Okefenokee swamp
Georgia/USA, November 1967

Heinrich Gohl (1926)
Shark River Slough, Everglades
Florida/USA, April 1981

Heinrich Gohl (1926)
Shark River Slough, Everglades
Florida/USA, April 1981

Christian Lichtenberg (1953)
Zedernwald, Haguro-san
Yamagata/Japan, 2001

Christian Lichtenberg (1953)
Cedar forest, Haguro-san
Yamagata/Japan, 2001

Jan Töve (1958)
Kiefern, Huang Shan-Berge 1
China, Oktober 1997

Jan Töve (1958)
Pines, Huang Shan Mountains 1
China, October 1997

Jan Töve (1958)
Kiefern, Huang Shan-Berge 2
China, Oktober 1997

Jan Töve (1958)
Pines, Huang Shan Mountains 2
China, October 1997

Graeme Matthews (1949)
Kiefern, Huang Shan
China, 1989

Graeme Matthews (1949)
Pines, Huang Shan
China, 1989

Jan Töve (1958)
Kiefern, Huang Shan-Berge 3
China, Oktober 1997

Jan Töve (1958)
Pines, Huang Shan Mountains 3
China, October 1997

Heinrich Gohl (1926)
Naabi-Hügel, Serengeti
Afrika, Dezember 1967

Heinrich Gohl (1926)
Naabi hills, Serengeti
Africa, December 1967

Eberhard Hummel (1939)
Toter Baum beim Gebirge Tassili n'Ajjer
Sahara/Algerien, November 1991

Eberhard Hummel (1939)
Dead tree near the Tassili n'Ajjer mountains
Sahara/Algeria, November 1991

Beat Presser (1952)
Affenbrotbaum–1
Morondava/Madagaskar, Juli 1992

Beat Presser (1952)
Baobab–1
Morondava/Madagascar, July 1992

Beat Presser (1952)
Affenbrotbaum–2
Tolagnara/Madagaskar, Juli 1992

Beat Presser (1952)
Baobab–2
Tolagnara/Madagascar, July 1992

Konrad Wothe (1952)
Affenbrotbäume
Morondava/Madagaskar, April 1989

Konrad Wothe (1952)
Baobabs
Morondava/Madagascar, April 1989

Beat Presser (1952)
Affenbrotbaum−3
Morondava/Madagaskar, Juni 1992

Beat Presser (1952)
Baobab−3
Morondava/Madagascar, June 1992

Heinrich Gohl (1926)
Silberweide
Schweiz, Oktober 1986

Heinrich Gohl (1926)
White Willow
Switzerland, October 1986

Heinrich Gohl (1926)
Urwald, Lake Manyara
Tansania/Afrika, Dezember 1967

Heinrich Gohl (1926)
Primeval forest, Lake Manyara
Tansiania/Africa, December 1967

Emil Schulthess (1913–1996)
Bergurwald, Ruwenzori
Kongo/Uganda, 1956

Emil Schulthess (1913–1996)
Mountain primeval forest, Ruwenzori
Kongo/Uganda, 1956

Emil Schulthess (1913–1996)
Urwald von Mazumbai
Tasmanien/Australien, 1956

Emil Schulthess (1913–1996)
Primeval forest of Mazumbai
Tasmania/Australia, 1956

153

Günter Ziesler (1939)
Bergwald, Mahale-Mountains, Mahale NP
Tansania, Juni 1996

Günter Ziesler (1939)
Mountain forest, Mahale-Mountains, Mahale NP
Tansania, June 1996

Günter Ziesler (1939)
Nebelwald an der Atlantikküste
Serra do Mar/Brasilien, September 1987

Günter Ziesler (1939)
Cloud forest at the Atlantic Coast
Serra do Mar/Brasil, September 1987

Ulrich Ackermann

Ulrich Ackermann (geboren 1947) absolvierte ursprünglich eine Fotografenlehre im Atelier Hugo Frutig, Bern. Der Spezialist für grossformatige Panoramaaufnahmen fotografiert bevorzugt Motive aus Landschaft, Natur und Reisen, aber auch Tiere und Menschen. Er findet diese auf seinen zahlreichen Reisen, aber auch in der Heimat. Seine Arbeiten sind von den Werken des Flugfotografen Georg Gerster und von Fred Mayer beeinflusst, so ist denn auch die Flugfotografie, die er sich nach einer Reise durch Alaska zu eigen gemacht hat, eines seiner bedeutenden Spezialgebiete. Ackermann hat sich die Fertigkeit erarbeitet, freihändig aus dem Flugzeug heraus zu fotografieren. Er verwendet für seine Bilder generell analoge Geräte, welche ihm nach eigener Aussage ein «viel bewussteres Fotografieren» ermöglichen. Seine spektakulären, dokumentarischen Bilder zeigen einen grossen Sinn für Dramatik und Inszenierung. So erstaunt es nicht, dass er jahrelang davon geträumt hat, einmal einen ganzen Berg fotografieren zu können, was ihm inzwischen mit seiner Hasselblad X-Pan (Format 24 x 65 cm) möglich ist. Eine besondere Faszination geht von seinen hochformatigen Fotografien aus, durch die Ulrich Ackermann eine ganz eigene, ungewohnte Bildwirkung erzielt. Als junger Mann hat er Freikurse in Malen und Zeichnen an der Kunstgewerbeschule Bern belegt und das Gespür für die Malerei kommt seinen Fotografien in erstaunlicher Weise zugute. So entstehen Bilder, die in jeder Beziehung unverwechselbar sind, was er in seinen eigenen Worten so ausdrückt: «Vorbilder sind gut und motivierend, aber schlussendlich sollte jeder seinem eigenen Bildgefühl nachgehen und es fotografisch einfach durchziehen, Kritik hin oder her, und so seine eigene Bild-Handschrift finden». Diese Bildhandschrift äussert sich auch deutlich in Ackermanns Fotografien von Bäumen, mit denen er den Mitmenschen für die Schönheiten der Natur die Augen öffnen und an die Verantwortung appellieren möchte, mit ihr bewusst und sorgsam umzugehen. Ackermann hat zahlreiche Bildbände veröffentlicht, unter anderem zu Alaska, St. Petersburg, Tansania und dem Greyerzerland, aber auch zu Braunbären und Schwänen. Seine Fotografien aus dem Greyerzerland wurden in Zusammenarbeit mit Ilford Imaging auch als vielbeachtete Ausstellung konzipiert und gezeigt.

Kontakt und Copyright Bild:
Ulrich Ackermann
Postfach 119, 3000 Bern 7, Schweiz
www.fotolangformat.ch

Ansel Adams

Am 20. Februar 1902 kam in San Francisco Ansel Easton Adams zur Welt. Nach einer schwierigen frühen Schulzeit liess Adams die staatlichen Bildungsinstitute bereits als Zwölfjähriger hinter sich, um seine Ausbildung autodidaktisch fortzusetzen. Ein Familienausflug in den Yosemite-Nationalpark 1916 hinterliess tiefe Eindrücke, die er in Fotografien im damals üblichen piktorialistischen Stil festzuhalten suchte. Seine Begeisterung für die Natur führte ihn 1919 in den dem Naturschutz verschriebenen Sierra Club, dessen Direktorium er von 1934 bis 1971 angehören sollte. Sein Ziel war jedoch die Ausbildung zum Konzertpianisten, 1925 schaffte er sich dafür einen Flügel an. Schon kurz darauf kam er jedoch mit Fotografien von Paul Strand in Kontakt, die ihn derart beeindruckten, dass er sich intensiver der Fotografie zu widmen begann. Noch lange Zeit wurde Adams zwischen dem Wunsch, Musiker zu werden und seiner Karriere als Fotograf hin und her gerissen. 1930 lernte er Paul Strand persönlich kennen, dessen präzise Vorstellungen von guter Fotografie dazu führten, dass er sich 1932 mit Edward Weston, Imogen Cunningham, John Paul Edwards, Sonya Noskowiak, Henry Swift und Willard van Dyke zur Gruppe f/64 zusammenschloss. Die Bezeichnung der Gruppe leitet sich von der damals kleinstmöglichen Blendenöffnung ab, welche eine gleichmässige Schärfentiefe vom Vordergrund zum Hintergrund der Fotografie ermöglicht und so zum angestrebten Ideal der Gruppe, maximaler Detailgenauigkeit, führt. Seine zahlreichen Ausflüge nach Yosemite beinhalteten auch einige Erstbesteigungen, wodurch einmalige Dokumente der noch von Menschenhand unberührten Natur entstanden. 1937 vernichtete ein Atelierbrand tausende Negative aus dem Frühwerk Adams. Gegen Ende der 1930er-Jahre entwickelte er sein berühmtes «Zonensystem», welches seither als das rigoroseste und ausgefeilteste System für die Kontrolle des Konstrastumfangs in der Schwarz-Weiss-Fotografie gilt. Es ermöglicht, die Kontrastwerte des Motivs ideal in das Raster des möglichen Kontrastumfangs des verwendeten Filmmaterials zu übersetzen. So entstanden zur technischen Perfektion gebrachte Negative, welche beliebig vergrössert werden konnten. Dank seinem Zonensystem konnte Adams die einzelnen tonalen Werte manipulieren und so die motivische Gewichtung innerhalb des Bildes grundlegend verändern. Ein Ergebnis seiner Obsession mit der fotografischen Technik war ein erstes Lehrbuch, «Making a Photograph», welches 1935 herauskam. «The Basic Photo Series», erschienen 1948–1956, löste die fotografische Arbeit aus dem experimentellen Kontext und erlaubte dem Laien erstmals, dank einer klaren Arbeitsanweisung konsistent hervorragende Abzüge herzustellen. 1940 führte Adams den ersten der später legendären «Yosemite-Workshops» durch, das «U.S. Camera Photographic Forum» mit Edward Weston. 1952 half er mit, das Magazin «Aperture» zu gründen und im Jahre 1958 wurde ihm der bereits dritte «Guggenheim Grant» zur Dokumentierung der Nationalparks der USA zugesprochen. Adams Bekanntschaft und Zusammenarbeit mit dem Erfinder des Sofortbildverfahrens «Polaroid», Edwin Land, sind zahlreiche bemerkenswerte Farbbilder zu verdanken. 1963 erhielt Adams zusammen mit Nancy Newhall den Auftrag, die Universität Kalifornien fotografisch zu dokumentieren. Die unter dem Titel «Fiat Lux» entstandene Arbeit gehört zu seinen Hauptwerken. 1966 wurde er zum Fellow der «American Academy of Arts and Sciences» ernannt; 1980 erhielt er aus den Händen von Präsident Jimmy Carter die «Freedom Medal», die höchste zivile Auszeichnung der Vereinigten Staaten. Am 22. April 1984 verstarb Ansel Adams in Carmel, Kalifornien. Er hinterliess seine Frau Virginia und seine zwei Kinder Michael und Anne. Zur Ehre seines Andenkens wurden 1984 «The Minarets Wilderness» im Inyo National Forest in «Ansel Adams Wilderness» umbenannt. Als weitere Ehrung wurde ein Jahr darauf der Mount Ansel Adams in der Sierra Nevada ausgeschieden. Wie kaum ein anderer hat Ansel Adams das fotografische Erbe des amerikanischen Westens geprägt. Eine ganze Generation von Fotografen baute auf seinen Arbeiten auf und fand Anregung in seiner überwältigenden technischen Brillanz, der seine tiefe Liebe zur Natur kontrastierend gegenübersteht. Adams vermochte, eine gewöhnliche Szenerie mit einer Leuchtkraft und Intensität wiederzugeben, welche insbesondere der Natur eine beinahe religiöse Expressivität einflösst und so hervorragend geeignet ist, Aspekte des Umweltschutzes hervorzuheben.

Kontakt und Copyright Bilder:
The Ansel Adams Gallery
Postfach 4185, Burlingane, CA 940111, USA
www.anseladams.com

Urs Martin Bachmann

Bereits als kleines Kind interessierte sich Urs Bachmann (geboren 1961) leidenschaftlich für die Natur. Schon damals verbrachte er seine Zeit am liebsten draussen im Wald. Mit seinem Vater, der mit einer alten Voigtländer-Kamera fotografierte, streifte er durch die noch weitgehend intakten Landschaften um Basel. Nicht weit von seinem damaligen Wohnort Muttenz begegnete er zahlreichen heute selten gewordenen Tieren, er beschreibt das Zusammentreffen mit einem Uhu und einem Auerhahn als magische Momente seiner Kindheit. Nach und nach weckte diese enge Beziehung mit der Natur in ihm das Bedürfnis, seine Eindrücke und seine Sichtweise mit der Kamera festzuhalten. Er begann damit, als er mit 17 Jahren auf einer Interrail-Reise Europa durchquerte. Kurz darauf führte ihn eine Weltreise nach Thailand, Malaysia, Bali, Australien, Neuseeland und in die Südsee, was ihm ermöglichte, nebst Landschaft, Flora und Fauna auch fremde Kulturen im Bild festzuhalten. Nach sieben Jahren intensiver Auseinandersetzung mit der Fotografie erschien 1994 seine erste internationale Publikation im renommierten Magazin «Animan». Im selben Jahr folgte eine Multivisions-Diaschau und 1997 konnte Urs Bachmann seinen ersten Bildband «Faszination Neuseeland» veröffentlichen. Während er in den Anfangsjahren vom Werk David Muenchs, Frans Lantings, Jim Brandenburgs oder Ansel Adams beeinflusst war, sind seine eigenständigen und originellen heutigen Arbeiten eher ein Ausdruck seiner Beschäftigung und geistigen Verwandtschaft mit Caspar David Friedrich. So fotografiert Bachmann bevorzugt in extremen Randstunden mit langen Belichtungszeiten, was die Konturen der Landschaft besonders hervorhebt. Mit dieser und anderen Techniken sucht er einen speziellen emotionellen Moment festzuhalten, der sinnbildlich für das Durchdrungensein mit der Natur steht. Hier spiegelt sich auch Bachmanns Überzeugung, dass der Mensch als Teil der Natur ein Gleichgewicht mit seiner Umwelt anstreben muss, um überleben zu können. Sein neuestes Buch, welches sich einer der wohl schönsten Gartenlandschaften der Welt, der Toskana widmet, erscheint voraussichtlich im Frühjahr 2008.

Kontakt und Copyright Bild:
Urs Bachmann
Breitweg 1, 4152 Gempen, Schweiz
www.bachmannurs.ch

Cornelia Dörr

Cornelia Dörr wurde 1963 in Chemnitz geboren. 1991 reiste sie nach Costa Rica, wo sie mit einer Praktika-Spiegelreflexkamera ihre Eindrücke festzuhalten suchte. Die Schwierigkeit, unter den extremen Lichtbedingungen des Regenwaldes zu fotografieren, brachte sie dazu, sich intensiver der Fotografie zu widmen. Besonders beeinflusst wurde sie durch die Werke von skandinavischen und amerikanischen Fotografen wie Hans Strand, Jan Töve, Art Wolfe oder David Muench. Heute arbeitet sie bevorzugt mit einer Nikon D2x sowie mit einer Hasselblad Panoramakamera. Cornelia

Dörrs dramatisch komponierte Bilder zeichnen sich durch eine besondere Vielfalt der eingesetzten Gestaltungselemente aus. Ihre meisterliche Beherrschung sich überlagernder und ergänzender Mittel, wie beabsichtigte Unschärfen, schlechtes Wetter, Abstraktionen und besondere Lichtstimmungen, erzeugen perfekte, ausdrucksstarke Inszenierungen, welche die Schönheit der Motive herausziselieren. Ab 1998 unternahm sie insgesamt vier Reisen nach Patagonien und den Anden. Die eindrücklichen Bilder der von Wind und Eis gezeichneten Landschaft Patagoniens sowie der kargen Hochebenen der Anden brachten Cornelia Dörr und ihrem Mann Ramon, der ebenfalls leidenschaftlich fotografiert, zahlreiche internationale Anerkennungen ein, so 2000 den BG Wildlife Photographer of the Year Award, 2001 den Nature's Best Magazine Award, 2002 den 1. Platz im Europäischen Naturfotowettbewerb sowie 2004 den Gerald Durrell Award. 2004 erschien ein Bildband mit ihren Arbeiten aus Patagonien, welche zudem mit einer Panoramaaufnahme des Grey-Gletschers (im Chilenischen Nationalpark Torres del Paine) in der Photographer's Hall of Fame besonders geehrt wurden. Cornelia Dörrs persönliches Anliegen ist es, mit ihren Bildern dem Publikum die Faszination der Natur zugänglich zu machen, Begeisterung und Staunen zu wecken und es so dafür zu gewinnen, sich für den Erhalt und den Schutz des «Wunders Natur» einzusetzen. Cornelia Dörr lebt und arbeitet als freiberufliche Fotodesignerin in Düsseldorf.

Kontakt und Copyright Bilder:
Cornelia Dörr
Eisenstruckstr. 5a, 9114 Chemnitz, Deutschland
www.doerr-naturbilder.de

Heinrich Gohl

Bereits als Achtjähriger hat Heinrich Gohl (geboren 1926) im Garten seines Elternhauses die ersten Naturfotografien gemacht – ein Erlebnis, das ihn ebenso prägte, wie die sonntäglichen Waldspaziergänge mit seinem Vater. Doch erst viel später sollte ihn die Naturfotografie als Berufung in ihren Bann ziehen. Nach einer Ausbildung zum Innenarchitekten zog ihn das Fernweh 1952 zunächst für ein Jahr nach Afrika. Unter den Eindrücken eines längeren Aufenthalts in Alaska entschied er sich schliesslich definitiv für die Fotografie. 1967 erschien Gohls erster Bildband, «Ein Tag in der Steppe», der seither von 25 weiteren, in 9 Sprachen übersetzten Publikationen gefolgt wurde. Obwohl seinen frühen Bildern oftmals die Prägung durch Vorbilder wie Ansel Adams oder Ernst Haas anzusehen ist, weisen

bereits die ersten Arbeiten eine ganz eigen geartete Emotionalität auf, die sich wie eine künstlerische DNS durch alle seine Werke zieht. Gohl selbst erläutert die Ursache dieser Eigenständigkeit mit der Liebe zur Sache: «Ich habe, so sieht es ja wohl aus, mein Leben lang diese früh erworbene Zuneigung [zum Wald] behalten und die damit zusammengehende Empfindsamkeit, die mir bis heute jede Gleichgültigkeit verbietet». Man darf also durchaus von einer gewissen Besessenheit sprechen, die Heinrich Gohl umtreibt. Und so erstaunt es nicht, dass er wesentliche künstlerische Einflüsse bei anderen besessenen Kreativen findet, wie beispielsweise Caspar David Friedrich, Jasper Johns, Ludwig van Beethoven oder George Gershwin. Sie alle hatten es nicht nötig, sich zur Erlangung eines Wiedererkennungswertes an äusserliche Gestaltungsmerkmale zu halten. Die Unverwechselbarkeit war ja als Ausdruck ihrer Persönlichkeit ohnehin gegeben und jeder Formalismus hätte zwangshaft und gekünstelt die Entfaltung eingeengt. Heinrich Gohl ist da keine Ausnahme. Denn obwohl seine Bilder alle eine unverkennbare Handschrift tragen, kommt diese nicht durch einen bestimmten Blickwinkel, bestimmte Techniken oder andere Gestaltungsmerkmale zustande. Es ist vielmehr die Haltung des Fotografen, welche sich atmosphärisch auf die Betrachter überträgt. Mit zunehmender Reife nimmt denn bei ihm auch die Sublimierung des atmosphärisch erfassten, einmaligen Augenblicks zu. So hat in seinen neueren Werken der gewählte Ausschnitt kaum noch Bedeutung für die Wirkung der Bilder. Ihm gelingt damit bravourös, jenseits von sich anbiedernder Fotogenität den Blick für das Besondere im vermeintlich Gewöhnlichen zu vermitteln. Als Initiator und Gestalter der Ausstellung «Wälder der Erde» geht ein langgehegter Wunsch Heinrich Gohls in Erfüllung, den er mit Ausdauer und Verve über Jahrzehnte hinweg vorangetrieben hat. Gleichzeitig äussert sich darin eine Sublimierung seines Lebenswerks, das mit dieser konzentrierten Vermittlung der Kraft und Formen von Bäumen und Wäldern eine weitere Verdichtung findet.

Kontakt und Copyright Bilder:
Heinrich Gohl
Arabienstrasse 5, 4059 Basel, Schweiz
www.wald-klima-umwelt.ch

Ernst Haas

Der aus Österreich stammende Ernst Haas kam am 2. März 1921 in Wien zur Welt. Der vielseitig begabte junge Mann widmete sich der Malerei, der Schauspielerei sowie dem Film, begann dann jedoch ein Medizinstudium, das er 1947 abbrach. Sein grosses Interesse an der Fotografie hatte ihn kurz nach dem Krieg eine Kamera gegen Nahrungsmittel eintauschen lassen, dies trotz des eigenen nagenden Hungers! Um sein neues Gerät beherrschen zu lernen, meldete er sich an der graphischen Lehr- und Versuchsanstalt in Wien zu einem Kurs an, wo er jedoch zu Beginn wegen «Talentlosigkeit» abgewiesen wurde. Er fand zu seinem Thema, als ihm der Schriftleiter der Zeitschrift «Der Film» den Rat gab, anstatt Landidyllen doch das Zeitgeschehen im kriegsversehrten Europa zu dokumentieren. 1946 wurde seine erste, eigenwillige Reportage über eine Armenspeisung gedruckt, die von den Verantwortlichen der Zeitschrift «Heute» bemerkt wurde. «Heute» war das Organ der amerikanischen Besatzungsmacht und fortan konnte Haas für beide Zeitschriften als freier Fotojournalist arbeiten. Seine Aufnahmen von Kriegsgefangenen aus Russland brachten ihm schliesslich den internationalen Durchbruch. Die eindrücklichen und erschütternden Bilder wurden nicht nur von «Heute» abgedruckt, sondern auch vom Internationalen Roten Kreuz zur Familienzusammenführung verwendet. «Life» druckte nachträglich einen Grossteil der Reportage nach und dies war der Auslöser dafür, dass Haas von den Gründern der Fotoagentur «Magnum» aufgefordert wurde, ihrem Kreis beizutreten. 1950 wurde er Vollmitglied von «Magnum», 1958 Vizepräsident und 1960 Präsident der Agentur. Seine intensiven Experimente mit dem neuartigen Kodachrome Farbfilmmaterial brachten ihm Anfang der 1950er-Jahre den Auftrag ein, für «Life» das Leben in New York zu dokumentieren. Die 1953 veröffentlichte Serie war eine Sensation, die ihre Fortsetzung in Reportagen wie «The Magic of Colours in Motion» fand. Diese bahnbrechende Sportreportage beinhaltete zuvor noch nie gesehene Effekte wie Bewegungsunschärfen und überlagerte Filme. Zahlreiche Städtereportagen folgten und 1962 zeigte das Museum of Modern Art eine vielbeachtete Einzelausstellung von Haas' Werken. Neben zahlreichen Buchprojekten erschien in den 1960er-Jahren auch sein Film «The Art of Seeing», der mit einer von Kodak geförderten Wanderausstellung dokumentiert wurde und später einer von ihm geleiteten Sendefolge im Fernsehen den Titel gab. 1964 entstand eine Fotostrecke für John Hustons Film «The Bible». Einige der herausragenden Bilder dieses Auftrags wurden von Haas 1971 im Bildband «The Creation» veröffentlicht. Der Film und die audiovisuelle Technik sollten zeitlebens eines seiner Steckenpferde bleiben. Aber auch die Landschaftsfotografie hatte es ihm angetan, wenig bekannt ist, dass er auch für die grandiosen und stilbildenden Fotografien aus den «Marlboro»-

Werbekampagnen verantwortlich zeichnete. In den 1970er-Jahren wurden zunehmend Blumen zu Haas' zentralem Motiv, die multimediale «Flower Show» von 1983 ist ein Höhepunkt seines Spätwerks. Kurz vor seinem Tod am 12. September 1986 in New York wurde er mit dem Hasselblad Award geehrt. Haas' besonderer Platz in der Geschichte der Fotografie erklärt sich aus seinem experimentellen Umgang mit der Farbfotografie, wo er bahnbrechende Arbeit geleistet hat. Sein sensationeller, flirrender Farbfotostil wandelte sich in den 1970er-Jahren zunehmend zu einem stilleren, aber auch präziseren Ausdruck, der sich besonders in seinen Büchern zum Zen-Buddhismus (Himalayan Pilgrimage, 1978) äussert. Seine ungekünstelte ethische Einstellung zur Fotografie wird besonders in seinen eigenen, markigen Aussprüchen deutlich: «Ich bin nicht daran interessiert, neue Motive abzulichten – ich möchte die Dinge neu sehen». «Mit der Fotografie wurde eine neue Sprache kreiert. Zum ersten Mal ist es jetzt möglich, Realität mittels Realität auszudrücken». «Meine Theorie der Komposition? Ganz einfach: den Auslöser erst dann betätigen, wenn sich alles im Sucher am richtigen Platz befindet!» Diese direkte, unverblümte und moderne Sichtweise findet ihren Ausdruck auch darin, dass Haas nicht viel vom Markendogmatismus hielt, den manche seiner Kolleginnen und Kollegen pflegten: «Die Kamera macht keinen Unterschied. Alle nehmen das auf, was man sieht. Aber man muss eben sehen!»

Kontakt und Copyright Bilder:
Estate of Ernst Haas
c/o Silverstein Photography
535 West 24th Street
New York, NY 10011 USA
www.ernst-haas.com

Mike Hill

Mike Hill (geboren 1949 in England) benutzte die Fotografie ursprünglich bloss als Hilfsmittel für sein eigentliches Interesse, die Naturgeschichte. Seine fotografische Karriere begann mit einer Zenith Photosniper, die er für Schwarz-Weiss-Aufnahmen von Vögeln nutzte. Auch wenn diese frühen Gehversuche seinen Ansprüchen nicht gerecht wurden, begann er sukzessive damit zu experimentieren, seine Interpretation der Natur in die dokumentarischen Aufnahmen einfliessen zu lassen. Seine Stilfindung wurde von den Werken Ernst Haas' und Jim Brandenburgs beeinflusst und mündete in eine besondere Bildsprache mit hohem Wiedererkennungswert. Typisch für Mike Hill ist eine Kombination von sorgfältig gewählter

Verschlussgeschwindigkeit und motivischer Komposition, die in dramatischen Bildern resultiert, welche einen sehr direkten und emotionalen Zugang zur Natur eröffnen. Der Geist der Orte und der Charakter der Tiere werden den Betrachtern lebendig in Erinnerung gerufen, da Hill aus den fotografierten Szenen Details herauszuarbeiten vermag, welche dem ungeschulten Auge in freier Wildbahn nicht auffallen würden. Auch die Musik und die Malerei haben ihn beeinflusst, was in seinen sorgsam ausbalancierten Bildern, die wie «Malereien mit Licht» erscheinen, deutlich wird. Zu seinen bedeutendsten Leistungen zählen zweifelsohne sechs Fotobücher, wobei diejenigen zum Arabischen Golf und dem Mittleren Osten besonders bekannt sind. Sein lebenslanges Suchen nach der Schönheit der Natur brachte ihm auch 14 Preise im «Wildlife Photographer of the Year»-Wettbewerb ein. Er benutzt eine 35 mm und eine 6 x 17 cm-Panoramakamera und bevorzugt die Arbeit mit der digitalen Ausrüstung. Hills Interesse für die Erhaltung der Umwelt ist einer der Hauptmotivationsfaktoren für seine Arbeit. Das zeigt sich nicht nur darin, dass seine Bilder massgeblich daran beteiligt waren, die Achtsamkeit von Bürgern und Behörden gegenüber Flora und Fauna im Mittleren Osten drastisch zu erhöhen. Es wird auch in seinem neuesten Projekt deutlich, das sich mit fotografischen Interpretationen der besonderen Atmosphäre des Dartmoores in Grossbritannien befasst.

Kontakt und Copyright Bild:
Mike Hill
The White Trillium, Stevenstone, Torrigton
Devon EX38 7HY, Great Britan
www.mikehillimages.com

Eberhard Hummel

Eberhard Hummel (geboren 1939) gehört zu den profiliertesten Naturfotografen Europas. Seine fotografische Karriere begann er, als er heimlich seine Lehrer im Schulunterricht ablichtete. Die Liebe zur Natur lässt ihn eine möglichst unverfälschte Wiedergabe der ausgewählten Bildausschnitte anstreben. Aufenthalte in Nordafrika, Südamerika, der Antarktis und ausgedehnte Reisen in der Sahara wirkten prägend auf sein Werk, das auch vom amerikanischen Fotografen David Muench beeinflusst wurde. Regelmässige Beiträge in Bildbänden, Kalendern und verschiedenen Zeitschriften zeigen, wie sehr sich Hummel in die unterschiedlichen Landschaftsformen und -charaktere einfühlen kann. Dies gilt auch für seine Tierportraits, die sich durch eine ausserordentliche Direktheit und Unmittelbarkeit auszeichnen.

Eberhard Hummel versteht es, den besonderen Augenblick so einzufangen, wie er sich dem Betrachter darbietet – ohne dabei zur Dramatisierung Zuflucht zu nehmen. So vermag er, die Schönheit der Natur ungekünstelt wiederzugeben, ein Beitrag dazu, jeden Einzelnen zum Schutz und zum Erhalt derselben zu animieren.

Kontakt und Copyright Bild:
Eberhard Hummel
Rüderer Strasse 13, 73733 Esslingen, Deutschland
www.naturbilder.de/EberhardHummel/

Frans Lanting

Frans Lanting (geboren 1951 in Rotterdam) gehört zu den bedeutendsten Naturfotografen unserer Zeit. Seine einflussreichen Bilder erscheinen weltweit in Büchern, Magazinen und Ausstellungen. Seit mehr als zwei Jahrzehnten dokumentiert er unsere Beziehung mit der Natur in unterschiedlichen Lebensräumen, vom Amazonas bis hin zur Antarktis. Er portraitiert Tiere als Botschafter für die Erhaltung vollständiger Ökosysteme und seine Publikationen tragen massgeblich dazu bei, das Bewusstsein für gefährdete ökologische Schätze zu schärfen. Lanting arbeitet regelmässig für die National Geographic Society, für deren Magazin er sowohl nach den legendären Bonobos in Zentralafrika gesucht, aber auch in einer spektakulären Aktion Südgeorgien umsegelt hat. Lantings neueste Werke behandeln ökologisch besonders bedeutende und sensitive Orte der Welt, beispielsweise die Vulkane Hawaiis, aber auch das Luangwa Valley in Zambia. Seine Bücher erhielten zahlreiche Preise und Auszeichnungen: «Niemand kann Tiere sosehr in Kunst verwandeln, wie Frans Lanting» urteilt zum Beispiel «The New Yorker». Unter seinen bedeutendsten Publikationen finden sich Klassiker der Naturfotografie: Jungles (2000), Penguin (1999), Living Planet (1999), Eye to Eye (1997), Bonobo, The Forgotten Ape (1997), Okavango: Africa's last Eden (1993), Forgotten Edens (1993) und Madagascar, A World Out of Time (1990). In den letzten Jahren arbeitete Lanting weltweit mit so unterschiedlichen Wissenschaftlern wie Paläobiologen und Astrophysikern zusammen, um sein neuestes Projekt «Life, A Journey Through Time» herauszubringen. Dabei handelt es sich um seine persönliche Interpretation der Evolution der Erde. Für seine engagierte Arbeit durfte Frans Lanting zahlreiche bedeutende Ehrungen entgegennehmen. So wurde er 2001 von seiner königlichen Hoheit, Prinz Bernhard, zum «Knight of the Golden Ark» geschlagen, der höchsten Auszeichnung für Umweltschutz der Niederlande. Auch World Press Photo

ehrte Lanting verschiedentlich, weiter hielt er den Titel des «BBC Wildlife Photographer of the Year» inne und der Sierra Club verlieh ihm den «Ansel Adams Award». 1999 nahm die Londoner Royal Photographic Society Frans Lanting in ihre Reihen auf. Er ist zudem Mitglied des Gründungsgremiums der «University of California» in Santa Cruz und des National Councils des World Wildlife Fund (WWF). Zudem führt er eine regelmässig erscheinende Kolumne in «The Outdoor Photographer». Frans Lanting lebt zusammen mit seiner Frau Christina Eckstrom, die eng mit ihm zusammenarbeitet, in Santa Cruz.

Kontakt und Copyright Bilder:
Frans Lanting Photography
207 McPherson Street, Suite D
Santa Cruz, CA 95060 USA
www.lanting.com

Christian Lichtenberg

Christian Lichtenberg wurde 1953 in Basel geboren. Längere Reisen und Auslandaufenthalte führten ihn nach Japan, in die USA, nach Afrika und nach Brasilien. Seit 1982 besteht sein eigenes Fotostudio in Basel. Neben zahlreichen anderen Auszeichnungen erhielt er 1983 den Grossen Preis der Biennale in São Paulo, Brasilien. «Zen oder die Kunst des Abdrückens» – so umschreibt Christian Lichtenberg den Entstehungsprozess seiner Kunst, jenen reduzierten, verinnerlichten Bildern, die nicht bloss Aus- und Ansichten sind, sondern eben auch Einsichten vermitteln. Das «Malen mit Licht» führt ihn dabei weit hinein in die jahrtausendealten atavistischen Fragen der Menschheit nach Sinn und Zweck, die schon deswegen nicht beantwortet werden können, weil dem Menschen kein feineres Instrument zur Kontemplation zur Verfügung steht, als das eigene Hirn. Während zwanzig Jahren hat sich Lichtenberg mit Schwarz-weiss-Fotografie auseinandergesetzt, durch die er subjektiv aus dem kollektiven Unterbewusstsein schöpfende ikonographische Bildkompositionen zu vermitteln suchte. Diese Phase gipfelte in der Ausstellung «My Private Universe» und wurde durch eine weniger anekdotisch gefärbte Bildsprache abgelöst, die sich zunehmend der Farbfotografie bediente. Lichtenberg nutzte diese Entwicklung, um sich auch dem Wesen der Natur zu nähern, wobei die Erkennbarkeit der Motive sekundär bleibt. Trotz dieser kombinierten Reflektion von Innen- und Aussenwelten bleibt die Persönlichkeit Lichtenbergs beim «Abdrücken» stets präsent. Seine Bilder sind so von einem selbstverständlichen Gestaltungswillen geprägt, dessen Stringenz sich dem Betrachter, der sich auf das Bild einlässt, erschliesst.

Die sich so einstellende besondere Verbundenheit und Identifikation mit dem Motiv ist wohl ein Grund dafür, dass Christian Lichtenbergs Bilder die Menschen so zu berühren und zu bewegen vermögen.

Kontakt und Copyright Bild:
Christian Lichtenberg
Schanzenstr. 46, 4056 Basel, Schweiz
www.lichtenberg.ch

Patrick Loertscher

Patrick Loertscher (geboren 1964 in Bern) zählt zu den erfolgreichsten und innovativsten Naturfotografen Europas. Sein Interesse an der Fotografie wurde schon früh durch Fotoreportagen in Magazinen wie National Geographic, Geo oder Merian geweckt. Doch auch die Modefotografien in Vogue und Vanity Fair übten eine grosse Faszination auf ihn aus. So fasste er schon in der Grundschule den Entschluss, Fotograf zu werden. Nach einem Volontariat im Schweizer Verlagshaus Ringier begann er eine Lehre als Fotolithograf an der Kunstgewerbeschule Bern. Schon damals und auch später als angestellter Fotolithograf unternahm er zahlreiche Reisen nach Asien, Australien und Neuseeland, auf denen er sich das Genre der Landschaftsfotografie erschloss. 1994 gründete Patrick Loertscher seinen eigenen Verlag, den er kürzlich mit der Patrick Loertscher Wilderness Gallery im appenzellischen Heiden ergänzt hat. Sein breites technisches Wissen ermöglicht ihm, auch grosse Formate selbst zu produzieren. Aufgrund seines Werdegangs erstaunt es nicht, dass er die analoge Technik bevorzugt. Loertschers dramatisch inszenierte Bilder zeugen von seiner Suche nach einzigartigen Stimmungen, welche sich drastisch von der Postkartenidylle behäbiger Schönwetterbilder abheben. Darin wird auch seine Beeinflussung durch das farbgewaltige Werk Art Wolfes deutlich, was in Kombination mit Loertschers Einfühlungsvermögen in die Formen der fotografierten Landschaftseindrücke zu einer besonders harmonischen Symbiose führt. Seine Fähigkeit, dem Charakter unterschiedlicher Naturräume präzise auf den Grund zu gehen, liegt wohl in der kenntnisreichen Durchdringung seiner Motive begründet. So erklärt sich auch seine Passion, die Eindrücke aus der Wildnis anderen Menschen weiterzugeben. Neben zahlreichen Kalendern hat Patrick Loertscher auch zwei bedeutende Bildbände über die Naturwunder Europas und Neuseelands publiziert.

Kontakt und Copyright Bilder:
Patrick Loertscher
Quellenweg 3, 9410 Heiden, Schweiz
www.patrickloertscher.com

Graeme Matthews

Graeme Matthews wurde 1949 in Blenheim, Neuseeland geboren. Sein Interesse an Fotografie wurde durch eine Kodak Brownie-Kamera ausgelöst, die er in einem Schrank im Haus seiner Eltern gefunden hatte. Diese nahm er auf ausgedehnte Fahrradausflüge ins Umland mit, wobei er seine ersten Erfahrungen mit der Landschaftsfotografie sammelte. 1983 kam seine erste grosse Publikation heraus, «The Edge of the Land», ein Buch über die Küste Neuseelands. Graeme Matthews wurde stark von Ansel Adams beeinflusst, aber er nennt auch Ernst Haas' Buch «The Creation» als bedeutende Inspirationsquelle für die Entwicklung seines fotografischen Auges. Sein künstlerisches Empfinden wird jedoch ebenso durch Musik geprägt, er interessiert sich vorwiegend für klassische Musik, Jazz, Blues und Country. Matthews Liebe zur Natur führte zu seinem bedeutendsten Auftrag, der darin bestand, in über 44 Ländern Bäume zu fotografieren, die in ein grossangelegtes Buchprojekt Eingang fanden. Dieses für ihn exemplarische Projekt passt ausgezeichnet zum Ziel, das er mit seiner Fotografie verfolgt: «Ich möchte die Schönheit der Natur aufzeigen und den Leuten die Notwendigkeit vor Augen führen, sich um die Natur zu kümmern.» Matthews benutzt im Gegensatz zu den meisten kontemporären Fotografen keine Digitaltechnik, aber eine breite Palette unterschiedlicher Kameras, was seinen dokumentarischen Stil hervorhebt. Er lebt mit seiner Frau Jenny, mit der er eng zusammenarbeitet, an der Küste Neuseelands, einem der schönsten Landstriche der Welt und gleichzeitig einer der bedeutenden künstlerischen Inspirationsquellen seines Werkes.

Kontakt und Copyright Bilder:
Graeme R. Matthews
Rarangi, R.D. 3, Blenheim New Zealand
www.graeme-matthews.com

Klaus Nigge

Klaus Nigge (geboren 1956) nutzte die Fotografie ursprünglich hauptsächlich für die Dokumentation seiner Beobachtungen im Tierreich. Er studierte Philosophie, Kunst und Biologie, ein Fachgebiet, das er später mit dem Schwerpunkt Botanik/Vegetationskunde vertiefte. Mit etwa 28 Jahren fiel ihm zunehmends auf, dass sich das Erlebte und Gesehene durch den Einsatz fotografischer Mittel in seiner Wirkung und Intensität steigern lässt. 1994 machte sich Klaus Nigge als Fotograf selbstständig. 1997 publizierte er sein erstes Buch, «Kamchatka – Adler, Bären und Vulkane». 1999 brachte National Geographic einen Artiel über

Riesenseeadler heraus, der den Beginn einer andauernden Zusammenarbeit mit dem renommierten Magazin markierte. Im selben Jahr kam ein weiteres Buch heraus, das ebenfalls den Adlern gewidmet war und 2004 publizierte er «Die Rückkehr des Königs» – Wisente in Polens Urwäldern. Weiter arbeitet Klaus Nigge regelmässig mit Magazinen wie Geo, Terre Sauvage und Arione zusammen, zudem hat er zahlreiche Preise und Auszeichnungen entgegengenommen, so den «Gerald Durrell Award» oder den «Wildlife Photographer of the Year». Nigges Bilder wirken auf den ersten Blick angenehm unaufgeregt, sie strahlen eine grosse innere Ruhe aus. Erst auf den zweiten Blick wird deutlich, wie sorgsam er dem Charakter der abgebildeten Tiere und deren Umgebung nachspürt. Es erstaunt nicht, dass er sich nachhaltig hat von den Bildern Hannu Hautalas, Frans Lantings, Michio Hoschinos oder Michael Nichols beeindrucken lassen. Das Einfangen von Atmosphäre ist für Nigge denn auch von zentraler Bedeutung: «Unsichtbares wie Gefühle, Klänge und Düfte zu fotografieren bzw. zu suggerieren, gehört zu den aufregendsten Herausforderungen». So sieht er auch Analogien zur Portraitfotografie, wo es weniger darum geht, dekorative bunte Bilder herzustellen, als die Persönlichkeit der abgebildeten Menschen herauszuarbeiten, ein Prozess, der für ihn auch in der Naturfotografie massgebend ist. Klaus Nigges Begeisterung für das Unverfälschte, Wahre und Echte verbindet sich hervorragend mit seinen umfassenden Kenntnissen aus Biologie, Kunst und Philosophie: Weder das zwanghaft Natürliche noch das aufdringlich Künstliche überwiegen in seinen ausgewogenen Bildern, mit denen er die Bedeutung von Tieren und Landschaften, der Umwelt und schliesslich auch der Erde herausarbeitet und den Menschen zur Beachtung anbietet.

Kontakt und Copyright Bild:
Klaus Nigge
Ernst-Becker-Strasse 12, 44534 Lünen
Deutschland
klaus.nigge@t-online.de

Beat Presser

Rar sind die Fotografen, denen der Sprung auf das internationale Parkett gelingt. Diesen Sprung ohne grössere Kompromisse zu vollziehen ist eigentlich unmöglich. Beat Presser (geboren 1952 in Basel) ist es gelungen, seinen persönlichen Interessen nachzugehen, seinen Projekten die nötige Reifezeit zu gewähren und einen umfassenden Blick auf das Metier des Fotografen zu bewahren,

ohne in die Falle der Spezialisierung – also Einschränkung – auf ein bestimmtes Motiv zu geraten. Die Vielseitigkeit seiner Arbeit beweist: Hier arbeitet jemand, der nicht zu einer gleichbleibenden Äusserlichkeit Zuflucht nehmen muss, um unverwechselbar zu sein. Unkategorisierbar spielt er in einer ganz anderen Liga, nämlich seiner eigenen. Dennoch zeichnen seine Bildkompositionen spezifische Merkmale aus. Die Spannung, welche Beat Pressers Bildern eigen ist, resultiert oftmals aus einer Konfrontation, die sowohl vom Motiv wie auch von der Belichtungstechnik herrühren kann. Andererseits durchzieht sein Werk ein Interesse an der Kraft der Abstraktion. Doch ist dies keine Abstraktion, die von der oberflächlich flotten Wirkung der letzlich eben doch schalen Leere herrührt. Pressers Abstraktion hebt hervor, macht Zusammenhänge deutlich und schafft ungemein reiche und üppige Bildkompositionen, die überwältigen können, öfters jedoch überwältigend introspektiv wirken. Hier zeigt sich der erfahrene Weltenbummler, der Vielgereiste, dem die Vermittlung von oftmals unter beschwerlichsten Bedingungen gewonnenen Eindrücken erstes Ziel bleibt. Denn diese Eindrücke führen zu sich selbst und Pressers Fotografien zeugen von dieser beschwerlichsten aller Reisen. Doch lässt er das Publikum nicht nur dadurch an seinem Weg teilhaben. Neben Gastprofessuren in Europa, Afrika, Südamerika und Asien organisiert er auch Ausstellungen und setzt sich besonders für die fotografische Ausbildung von Kindern und Jugendlichen ein. Angesichts der Eigenständigkeit Pressers Perspektive wird klar, dass er sich seinen ganz eigenen Zugang zur Fotografie gesucht hat. Schon mit sieben Jahren begann er zu fotografieren, das erste Bild – es zeigt einen Gartenzwerg neben einer Osterglocke – ist erhalten. Mit 15 sah er erstmals, wie sich ein Foto im Entwicklungsbad materialisiert. Das war der Moment, in dem Beat Presser den Entschluss fasste, Fotograf zu werden. Anfang der 1970er-Jahre konnte er bei den Modefotografen Onorio Mansutti in Basel sowie Just Jaeckin in Paris arbeiten. Während seiner Zeit in Paris nutzte er intensiv die Cinémathèque de France, die ihm die Welt des bewegten Bilds erschloss. In Paris war es auch, wo er den Film «Aguirre, der Zorn Gottes» sah und so erstmals in Kontakt mit dem Werk Werner Herzogs und Klaus Kinskis kam, was in ihm den Wunsch weckte, mit diesen Grössen des Films zusammenzuarbeiten. In Basel bildete er sich ab Mitte der 1970er-Jahre zum Kameramann aus, ab 1976 publizierte er zwei Jahre lang seine eigene Fotozeitschrift «The Village Cry», welche ihrer Zeit weit voraus war. Die Ausgabe 4/1977 enthält eine Reportage über Klaus Kinski und Daniel Schmid. Werner Herzog engagierte Beat Presser 1981 als Stand-fotograf und Kameraassistent für «Fitzcarraldo» und 1987 für «Cobra Verde». Im Rahmen dieser Projekte entstanden auch die weltbekannten Portraits von Klaus Kinski. In den folgenden Jahren schuf Beat Presser zahlreiche Dokumentar- und Kulturfilme. Ab 1988 arbeitete er zusammen mit Vera Pechel auf Madagaskar an einem Dokumentarfilm und an dem fotografischen Projekt «Vom Feuer zur Religion». Auch die in der Ausstellung gezeigte Serie «Baobab» entstand in diesem Zusammenhang. 1998 erschien sein Buch Alpentraum, eine Auseinandersetzung mit der Heimat. Danach begann er sich intensiv mit dem Buddhismus zu beschäftigen. Beginnend in Thailand arbeitete er fünf Jahre lang in Klöstern in Indien, Myanmar, Laos, Sri Lanka und Kambodscha. Daraus entstand das 2005 publizierte Buch «Oase der Stille», ein vorläufiger Höhepunkt im Bemühen Beat Pressers, atmosphärisch die Suche nach dem Echten und Wahren zu vermitteln.

Kontakt und Copyright Bild:
Beat Presser
Postfach 1845, 4001 Basel, Schweiz
www.beatpresser.com

Albert Renger-Patzsch

Im Jahr 1897 erblickte Albert Renger-Patzsch in Würzburg das Licht der Welt. Sein Vater Robert Renger-Patzsch war selbst ein begeisterter Amateurfotograf, der sich mit technischen Innovationen einen Namen gemacht hatte. Schon mit 14 Jahren beherrschte Albert zahlreiche fotografische Techniken, wie er sich selbst erinnerte: «Über die Technik des kombinierten Gummidrucks war ich mit vierzehn Jahren aufs Genaueste unterrichtet und fotografierte schon in allen Formaten mit den Apparaturen meines Vaters, allerdings ohne dessen Wissen.» Im Ersten Weltkrieg gelang es ihm, einer chemischen Zentralstelle des Generalstabs zugeteilt zu werden. 1919 nahm er ein Chemiestudium in Angriff, welches er 1921 abbrach, da er die Leitung des Bildarchivs des Folkwang-Verlags in Hagen übernehmen konnte. Ernst Fuhrmann, der Leiter des Folkwang- und Auriga-Verlags, erkannte die Talente Renger-Patzschs und regte die ersten Publikationen «Orchideen» und «Crassula» an. 1923 wechselte er zu einer Pressebildagentur und kurz darauf in die Buchhaltung einer Drogerie in Kronstadt (Rumänien), von wo ihn Ernst Fuhrmann jedoch wieder zurückholte. Ab 1925 schliesslich arbeitete Renger-Patzsch als selbstständiger Fotograf und gab das Buch «Das Chorgestühl von Cappenberg» heraus. Der Durchbruch kam mit dem 1928 publizierten Werk «Die Welt ist schön», eine der Grundlagen der modernen

Fotografie, das der «Neuen Sachlichkeit» in Deutschland zum Durchbruch verhalf. Albert Renger-Patzschs Fähigkeit, das Ästhetische und Schöne auch im industriellen Motiv hervorzuheben, brachte ihm zahlreiche Aufträge im Bereich der Industrie, Architektur und Werbung ein. 1929 wurden ihm im Folkwang-Museum in Essen Atelierräume zur Verfügung gestellt, 1933 übernahm er einen Lehrstuhl als Leiter der Fachabteilung «Bildmässige Fotografie» an der Folkwangschule. Jedoch verliess er diesen aufgrund von Differenzen mit den Nationalsozialisten schon nach zwei Semestern wieder. 1944 fiel sein Atelier einem Bombenangriff zum Opfer, bei dem auch das Archiv zerstört wurde. In der Folge siedelte er mit seiner Familie nach Wamel am Möhnesee um. Obwohl er weiterhin zahlreiche Industrieaufträge wahrnahm, fokussierte er sich nun laufend stärker auf die Naturfotografie. 1957 kam der Bildband «Landschaft zwischen Ruhr und Möhne» heraus, 1962 «Bäume» und 1966, dem Todesjahr Albert Renger-Patzschs, «Gestein». Sein Vermächtnis kann in seiner innovatorischen Bedeutung für die Fotografie kaum überschätzt werden. Renger-Patzsch hat als einer der ersten Fotografen überhaupt die Ästhetik industrieller Anlagen und Produkte wahrgenommen und bildlich festgehalten. Damit löste er einen noch heute andauernden Paradigmenwandel aus, galten doch die meisten seiner Motive den Zeitgenossen als nichtbildwürdig. Gleichzeitig emanzipierte er die Fotografie von der künstlerischen Malerei. Fotografie galt bis zur «Neuen Sachlichkeit» als minderwertiger Ersatz für Malerei, wovon die Techniken des gemalte Bilder imitierenden Piktorialismus zeugen. Getreu seinem Motto: «Überlassen wir die Kunst den Künstlern und versuchen wir mit den Mitteln der Fotografie Fotografien zu schaffen, die durch ihre fotografischen Qualitäten bestehen können» lotete Renger-Patzsch die der Fotografie innewohnenden Qualitäten in ganz neue Richtungen aus und fand so Motivbereiche, die mit anderen Mitteln nicht adäquat darstellbar waren. So hielt er selbst fest: «Dem starren Liniengefüge moderner Technik, dem luftigen Gitterwerk der Krane und Brücken, der Dynamik 1000-pferdiger Maschinen im Bild gerecht zu werden, ist wohl nur der Fotografie möglich.» Auch seine späten Baumfotografien zeugen stets von einem untrüglichen Blick für Strukturen und Oberflächen. Kontraste waren für Renger-Patzsch ein zu oberflächliches Mittel, um Spannung und Effekte zu erzielen. Er lotete vielmehr die delikaten Spannungsbögen zwischen Struktur und Oberfläche aus. Das führt zu vollkommen in sich ruhenden Bildern, denen jedoch jede kontemplative Langeweile abgeht, denn Dramaturgie und Grandezza rücken sich visuell unterschwellig nach und nach umso machtvoller ins Bewusstsein. 1957

verlieh ihm die Gesellschaft Deutscher Lichtbildner ihre David Octavius Hill-Medaille, die Biennale in Venedig ehrte ihn mit der Goldmedaille. Die Deutsche Gesellschaft für Fotografie zeichnete ihn 1960 mit dem Kulturpreis aus. 1961 erhielt er die Goldmedaille der Fotografischen Gesellschaft Wien und 1965 den Staatspreis des Kunsthandwerks des Landes Nordrhein-Westfalen.

Kontakt und Copyright Bild:
Archiv Ann und Jürgen Wilde
Niederberger Strasse 23, 53909 Zülpich, Deutschland
www.karl-blossfeldt-archiv.de

Norbert Rosing

Norbert Rosing wurde 1953 im Münsterland geboren. Als in der Volksschule im Fotounterricht Spiegelreflexkameras vorgeführt wurden, begeisterten ihn die sich ihm damit eröffnenden Möglichkeiten sosehr, dass er sich seine erste Kamera mit dem Aufstellen von Kegeln auf einer Kegelbahn finanzierte. Mit dieser zog er zuerst auf Wanderungen ins Umland von Berchtesgaden los, bald schon entdeckte er jedoch Skandinavien für sich, wodurch eine langanhaltende Faszination für die nordischen Länder geweckt wurde. 1988 stieg Rosing auf das Leica R-System um und begann das Projekt «Im Reich des Polarbären». Wie sich bald zeigen sollte, hatte er damit ein Motiv gefunden, welches er wie kein Zweiter in Szene zu setzen versteht. Rosing selbst meint: «Die Arktis ist für mich ein täglich neu sich öffnendes Buch mit tausenden von Seiten.» Seine inzwischen weltbekannten Fotografien von Eisbären führten ihn zu weiteren interessanten Projekten über Nationalparks in Deutschland und den USA (Yellowstone). 1992 wagte Rosing den Sprung in die Selbstständigkeit. Die Vielseitigkeit seiner Bilder ist immer wieder aufs Neue erstaunlich. Insbesondere seine Fähigkeit, über die Fotografie Atmosphäre und Gefühle auszudrücken, zieht die Betrachter seiner Bilder in ihren Bann. Dies umso mehr, als er kaum je auf Effekte aus ist, sondern mit Lichtstimmungen und Landschaftsformen arbeitet. So bezieht er auch in der Tierfotografie das Tier mit in die Landschaft ein oder betrachtet es als Teil davon. Rosing ist überzeugt, dass er seine Handschrift durch die Benutzung des Leica R-Systems gefunden habe. Dementsprechend bedeutsam ist ihm der technische Aspekt der Fotografie, wo er besonders die beinahe Dreidimensionalität erlangende Tiefe des Dias schätzt, die sich mit digitaler Technik nicht erreichen lässt. Seine Sorge um den Erhalt der authentischen Naturfotografie, die ohne digitale Bearbeitung auskommt, kennzeichnet auch seine ursprüngliche und natürliche Bildsprache, die bestens ohne überzogene Ästhetisierung auskommt. Rosings Bilder werden in zahlreichen Publikationen veröffentlicht, so publiziert er regelmässig in Geo sowie im National Geographic Magazine. Er hat sechs Bildbände veröffentlicht, je einen über die Nationalparks in Deutschland und Yellowstone, zwei über Polarbären, einer über Geparde sowie «Die Nacht ist wie ein stilles Meer», ein poetischer Bilderbogen. Er ist Mitglied der Deutschen Gesellschaft für Photographie, der Gesellschaft Deutscher Tierfotografen, der North American Nature Photography Association und der International League of Conservation Photographers. Darüber hinaus nimmt er als beratendes Mitglied von Polar Bears International besondere Verantwortung im Naturschutz wahr.

Kontakt und Copyright Bild:
Norbert Rosing
Amselweg 15, 82284 Grafrath, Deutschland
www.rosing.de

Hans-Peter Schaub

«Natur ist nie banal – immer anders», so umschreibt Dr. Hans-Peter Schaub (geboren 1961) seinen persönlichen Zugang zur Naturfotografie. Er führt sein Interesse an der Fotografie auf den Kunstunterricht am Gymnasium zurück, in dessen Rahmen er auch seine ersten Bilder gemacht hat. Nach einem Studium der Biologie und seiner Promovierung 1993 arbeitet er seit 1995 hauptberuflich als Fotojournalist. Sein erstes Buch, «Der Kaiserstuhl», erschien 2002. Seither hat Schaub zahlreiche weitere Publikationen herausgegeben, darunter einige Bildbände über den Schwarzwald sowie ein Buch über den Pfälzerwald. Zu seinen Vorbildern zählt er Frans Lanting, Ansel Adams, Shinzo Maeda, Henri Cartier-Bresson, Andreas Feininger und Galen Rowell. Schon im einleitend erwähnten Zitat wird Hans-Peter Schaubs Anspruch, die Fotografie als kreative Herausforderung zu begreifen, deutlich. Die naturnahen und atmosphärisch aufgeladenen Bilder spiegeln auch seine persönliche Haltung wider, durch die er sich zum Ziel setzt, Standpunkte zu beziehen und auszudrücken. Damit wirkt jedes einzelne Bild als Anregung, das Abgebildete zu reflektieren und sich darüber eine eigene Meinung zu bilden. Hier wird ein sozialer Beweggrund deutlich, der für die bildende Kunst allgemein zählt. Es überrascht nicht, dass sich Schaub nicht nur von anderen Fotografen, sondern auch von Musik und Malerei beeinflussen lässt, beispielsweise von den Werken William Turners, Caspar David Friedrichs, August Mackes oder auch Paul Cézannes. Dieser breiten Palette an unterschiedlichen Inspirationsquellen entspricht, dass er keinen grundlegenden Unterschied zwischen der Portrait- und der Landschaftsfotografie verspürt, denn so, wie sich Gesichtsausdrücke, Haltungen, Blicke verändern, sind auch die Landschaften einem kontinuierlichen Veränderungsprozess unterworfen. Hans-Peter Schaub selbst bringt es auf den Punkt, wenn er sagt: «Die Kunst ist bei beiden grossen Themen, im richtigen Moment auszulösen – wobei es meist nicht nur einen, sondern viele richtige Momente gibt.» Durch diesen sicheren Blick für die Alternative gelingt es Schaub, seine manchmal altbekannten Motive neu und ungewohnt in Szene zu setzen.

Kontakt und Copyright Bild:
Hans-Peter Schaub
Waldorfweg 41, 59063 Hamm, Deutschland
www.hanspeterschaub.de

Emil Schulthess

Emil Schulthess wurde am 29. Oktober 1913 in Zürich geboren. Nach einer Ausbildung zum Grafiker wurde er Hospitant beim Fotografen Hans Finsler an der Kunstgewerbeschule in Zürich. Die frühen 1930er-Jahre brachten ihn nach Paris, anschliessend machte er sich einen Namen als freischaffender Grafiker. Zahlreiche Arbeiten aus dem Bereich des Tourismus zeigen, wie hervorragend Schulthess den abstrahierenden grafischen Stil der Zeit zu handhaben verstand. 1937 heiratete er seine Frau Bruna und wurde Hausgrafiker beim Druck- und Verlagshaus Conzett Huber. Dort erschien ab 1941 die Monatszeitschrift «Du», wobei er zuerst deren grafische Gestaltung, später auch die Bildredaktion verantwortete. 1950 realisierte er das Projekt eines 360°-Panoramas der Sonnenbahn auf der Insel Hekkingen in Norwegen, ein Thema, das ihn zeitlebens beschäftigen sollte. Ab 1951 bis 1990 zeichnete Schulthess für die Gestaltung des Swissair-Kalenders verantwortlich. 1952 wurde er für das Mitternachtssonne-Panorama mit dem «US Camera Award» ausgezeichnet. Im Jahr darauf unternahm er eine Reise durch die USA, welche er 1955 in einem vielbeachteten Bildband dokumentierte. Für das 1957 herausgegebene Buch «Wildtiere im Kongo» sowie weitere Afrika-Publikationen unternahm Schulthess 1955/56 eine abenteuerliche Durchquerung des afrikanischen Kontinents. Die American Society of Magazine Photographers ehrte ihn für diese beiden Projekte 1958 mit ihrem «Annual Award». In den darauffolgenden Jahren bereiste er Japan, Hong-Kong sowie die Philippinen, was sich in prachtvoll illustrierten Büchern niederschlug, welche die Sinnlichkeit Ostasiens brillant einfangen. Anschliessend nahm er an einer Antarktis-Expedition der US-Navy und der National Science Foundation teil. Bereits 1960 wurden die so entstandenen Bilder im vielbeachteten Buch «Antarctica» veröffentlicht und in «Life» vorgestellt. Die Jahre 1960 bis 1962 brachten verschiedene Reisen nach Südamerika, was das Buchprojekt «Amazonas» zur Folge hatte. Verschiedene von Schulthess' Fotos wurden auch in der Ausstellung «Photography in Fine Arts» des Metropolitan Museum of Modern Art gezeigt. Carl Foremans Film «The Victors» bot Schulthess Gelegenheit, Portraits u.a. von Romy Schneider, Jeanne Moreau und George Hamilton herzustellen. 1964 erhielt er den Kulturpreis der Deutschen Gesellschaft für Photographie und im selben Jahr brach er bereits wieder auf grosse Reise auf, diesmal durch das kommunistische China. 1966 wurde der entsprechende Bildband lanciert, der mit einer Gesamtauflage von 50 000 Exemplaren auf ein enormes Echo stiess. Seine Arbeiten über Afrika und China brachten ihm 1967 den «US Camera Achievement Award» ein. 1969 und 1970 realisierte er ein 360°-Panorama von der Dufourspitze, welches zunächst an der Weltausstellung in Osaka gezeigt und darauf in zahlreichen Publikationen veröffentlicht wurde. Als Ergebnis zahlreicher Reisen hinter den Eisernen Vorhang erschien 1971 das Buch «Sowjetunion». Die im Westen als Sensation empfundenen Einblicke in die kommunistische Supermacht waren auf Anhieb ein grosser Erfolg. Im Jahr darauf ging Schulthess' einflussreiche und von Kodak unterstützte Wanderausstellung «Unspoiled Nature» in zahlreichen Ländern auf die Reise. In den 1970er Jahren beschäftigte sich Emil Schulthess zunehmend mit den technischen Problemen der Panoramatechnik, die er zur Vollendung entwickelte. So wurden 1974–1978 verschiedene Publikationen mit seinen Panoramaaufnahmen herausgegeben, die 1983 im Auftrag gipfelten, für das Asahi-Newspaper in Tokyo das Neujahrsblatt zu gestalten. Nie zuvor wurde einem Ausländer diese Ehre zuteil und Schulthess wurde der schwierigen Aufgabe mit einer 360°-Panoramaaufnahme von Mount Fuji gerecht. Im selben Jahr gewann sein Bildband «Swiss Panorama» die «Goldene Letter» als eines der schönsten Bücher der Welt. 1984 wurde die damals weltgrösste Farbvergrösserung mit den Ausmassen 82 x 7,2 m, auch dies ein Schulthess-Bild, für den Schweizer Pavillon an der Expo 85 hergestellt. «Landschaft der Urzeit», 1988 herausgegeben, sollte sein letztes grosses Publikationsprojekt werden. Emil Schulthess verstarb am 20. Januar 1996. Die Besonderheit seines Werks liegt im untrüglichen Geschmack seiner Bildkompositionen, die dem Auge auch nach vielfacher Betrachtung immer neue Aspekte erschliessen und sich so deutlich von den Werken anderer Landschaftsfotografen der Zeit absetzen. Schulthess hat es verstanden, mit seinen Bildern Herz und Auge des Betrachters gleichermassen zu erfreuen. Als Mittler zwischen den Kulturen erlaubten seine Publikationen erste, langersehnte Einblicke in Fremdes und Andersartiges. Die elegante Art und Weise, wie ihm dies gelungen ist, zeugt von der Liebe zum Menschen und den Wundern der Erde. In Anerkennung seiner Arbeit in der Antarktis wurde der Punkt 84°74' südlicher Breite und 115°00' westlicher Länge offiziell als «Schulthess Buttress» benannt.

Kontakt und Copyright Bild:
Emil Schulthess Erben, Photoarchiv
Zollikerstrasse 128, CH–8008 Zürich, Schweiz
www.emil-schulthess.ch

Hans Strand

Hans Strand kam 1955 zur Welt. Kurz nachdem er 1981 vom Royal Institute of Technology in Stockholm abging, begann er eine Karriere als Ingenieur. Nach neun Jahren in seinem Beruf entschied er, sich künftig vollumfänglich seinem Hobby, der Landschaftsfotografie, zu widmen. Zeitlebens fühlte er sich zur ungezähmten und unmanipulierten Seite der Natur hingezogen, so bereute er seinen Entschluss nie. «Die Wildnis ist die Mutter aller Dinge. Sie ist immer ehrlich und nie oberflächlich.» Diesem Grundsatz verpflichtet, begann er zuerst, die Landschaften Skandinaviens zu fotografieren und erschloss sich später den gesamten Planeten als Motiv. So fotografierte er von den unendlichen Weiten der Arktis bis hin zu dampfenden Regenwäldern und trockenen Wüsten jedes erdenkliche Panorama. Seine Arbeit ist in zahlreichen international anerkannten Magazinen erschienen und er hält Vorlesungen in Schweden und Übersee. 1995 kam sein erstes Buch «And the Sea Never Rests» heraus, 1998 gefolgt von «For as Long as the Forests Grow». Seine Fotografien zierten den internationalen Canon-Kalender 1999 und im selben Jahr erhielt er die «Nature of the Year»-Auszeichnung der Swedish Nature Protection Agency. 2001 gewannen seine Landschaftsfotografien im «The European Photographer of the Year»-Wettbewerb. Sein drittes Buch, «The Eighth Day» kam 2002 heraus. Das schwedische Fotomagazin FOTO verlieh ihm den Titel des «Nordic Photographer of the Year» 2003. Hans Strands neueste Publikation, «Arctic Impressions», wird 2007 an die Buchhändler ausgeliefert.

Kontakt und Copyright Bild:
Hans Strand
Hertgvägen 3, 12652 Hägersten, Schweden
www.hansstrand.com

Jan Töve

Jan Töve Johansson wurde 1958 in Boras (Schweden) geboren. Als er Schwarz-weiss-Fotografien seines Vaters sah, begann er sich für die Fotografie zu interessieren. Mit 12 Jahren gewann er in einem Preisausschreiben seine erste Kamera. Schon 1975 konnte er einen ersten öffentlichen Erfolg verbuchen, als er den von einem Jagdmagazin ausgelobten Fotowettbewerb für sich entscheiden konnte. Mehrfach wurde Töve zum «BBC Wildlife Photographer of the Year» gewählt, darüber hinaus zeichnete ihn das schwedische Magazin «Foto» 1995 mit dem Preis «Nordic Photographer of the Year» aus. Die schwedische Umweltschutzbehörde verlieh ihm den Titel «Nature Photographer of the Year» im Jahr 2003. Seit seinem ersten Buch «Speglingar», das 1996 erschien, hat Jan Töve zahlreiche weitere Publikationen herausgegeben, die weltweit auf grosse Anerkennung stiessen und viele Auszeichnungen gewannen. Ab 2001 arbeitete er an einem Dokumentationsprojekt entlang des Viskan-Flusses in Schweden. Die aus dieser Arbeit entstandenen Fotografien zeigen eindrücklich die Spannweite der ausgesprochen zeitgemässen Sichtweise Jan Töves. Er selbst sieht seine Motive stets als Landschaften – seien sie naturbezogen oder auch sozial. Menschen sind in seiner Fotografie so stets in ihrem natürlichen Umfeld beinahe wie zufällig mitabgebildet und konstituieren dadurch einen Teil der Landschaften Jan Töves. Dabei geht es ihm nicht so sehr um die Hervorhebung von kontrastierenden Eindrücken als vielmehr darum, diese Kontraste zu überbrücken und in einem Gesamtbild einzubetten. Damit zeigt er auf, wie sehr der Mensch mit den Zeugnissen seiner Zivilisation eben auch ein integraler Bestandteil der Landschaften auf der Erde ist. Jan Töve Johansson lebt und arbeitet als Landschaftsfotograf, Publizist und Autor in Schweden, wo er sich auch seinem Engagement in der Ausbildung von Fotografen widmet.

Kontakt und Copyright Bild:
Prästgården, Härna 150
523 99 Hökerum, Schweden
www.jantove.com

Christian Vogt

Christian Vogt (Basel 1946)
Seit 1970 fotografisch-visuelle Konzepte für sich selbst und im Auftrag. Bücher, Monografien, Kataloge und Ausstellungen.

Kontakt und Copyright Bild:
Studio Christian Vogt
Postfach 2226, CH–4001 Basel, Schweiz
www.christianvogt.com

Edward Weston

Edward Weston erblickte am 24. März 1886 in Highland Park, Illinois (USA) das Licht der Welt. Schon als Jugendlicher begann er sich für die Fotografie zu interessieren und mit 16 erhielt er seine erste Kamera, eine Kodak Bull's Eye No. 2, geschenkt. Seine Bilder waren derart erfolgreich, dass sie bereits ein Jahr darauf 1903 am Art Institute in Chicago ausgestellt wurden. Daraufhin betätigte er sich als Wanderfotograf und gelangte so bis nach Kalifornien, wo er sich um 1906 als Portraitfotograf niederliess. Drei Jahre später heiratete er seine erste Frau, Flora May Chandler, die ihm vier Söhne schenkte. Sein erstes Fotostudio konnte er 1911 in Tropica eröffnen; 1919 wurde er Mitglied des London Salon of Photography. In dieser Zeit begann sich Weston vom seinerzeit vorherrschenden Piktorialismus zu lösen, dessen Ziel eine möglichst «gemalte» und impressionistische Anmutung des fotografischen Portraits war. Weston wurde so zu einem der Begründer der «straight photography», die sich eine möglichst realistische Wiedergabe der fotografierten Motive zum Ziel setzte. Zusammen mit seiner Geliebten, der Fotografin Tina Modotti, reiste er 1923 nach Mexico City, wo er ein eigenes Studio betrieb. Fünf Jahre später kehrte er nach Kalifornien zurück und gründete ein Atelier in Carmel. Sukzessive führte er damals seinen Sohn Brett in die Fotografie ein, der seinen Vater im Atelier unterstützte. Zusammen mit Ansel Adams, Willard van Dyke, Imogen Cunningham und anderen gründete Weston 1932 in New York die Gruppe f/64. Der Begriff bezeichnet die kleinstmögliche Blendenöffnung der damaligen Grossformatkameras, welche in einer grösstmöglichen Schärfentiefe resultiert. Dadurch entstehen vom Vordergrund zum Hintergrund gleichmässig scharfe Bilder, die den Zielsetzungen der «straight photography» in idealer Weise entsprechen. Im Manifest der Gruppe heisst es denn auch, dass die Fotografie immer unabhängig von ideologischen Konventionen einer Kunst oder einer Ästhetik bleiben müsse. Als erster Fotograf überhaupt wurde Weston 1937 zum Guggenheim-Fellow ernannt. 1938 heiratete er seine Assistentin Charis Wilson. Die 1930er- und 1940er-Jahre waren eine äusserst produktive Zeit für ihn, so erschienen zahlreiche Bildbände, welche mit seinen Bildern illustriert sind. Darunter finden sich so bedeutende Werke wie «Leaves of Grass» nach Gedichten von Walt Whitman oder das Standardwerk «My Camera on Point Lobos». Die wilde Küste von Point Lobos war auch das Experimentierfeld für Westons erste Farbfotografien, die eindrücklich seine Versatilität demonstrieren. Instinktiv entwickelte er für seine farbigen Arbeiten einen ebenso eigenständigen Zugang zum Motiv, wie für seine Schwarz-Weiss-Bilder. Seine Versuche von 1947 kommentierte Weston selbst: «Wenn jemand behauptet, dass die Farbe irgendwann einmal Schwarzweiss in der Fotografie voll ablösen wird, redet er Unfug. Farbe und Schwarzweiss stehen nämlich nicht im Wettbewerb miteinander; es handelt sich um unterschiedliche Hilfsmittel zur Erreichung unterschiedlicher Ziele.» Parallel zu diesen Farbversuchen begann Willard van Dyke das Filmprojekt «The Photographer», in dem Edward Westons Arbeitsweise dokumentiert ist. Leider musste er die Farbexperimente im selben Jahr aufgrund seiner sich verschlimmernden Parkinson-Erkrankung aufgeben. Seine Söhne Brett und Cole sowie Bretts Frau Dody Warren stellten nach seiner Erkrankung unter seiner Anleitung Abzüge von rund 800 bedeutenden Aufnahmen her. In Anerkennung Westons herausragender Position in der amerikanischen Fotogeschichte wurde er 1951 zum Ehrenmitglied der American Photographic Society ernannt. Am 1. Januar 1958 verstarb Edward Weston in Carmel, Kalifornien. Durch technische Meisterschaft gelang es ihm, Bilder von ungewöhnlichem Strukturreichtum zu kreieren, die dem Betrachter die Schönheit und Finesse auch einfachster Objekte vor Augen führen. Westons Tagebücher verdeutlichen, zu welch hohem Preis diese vermeintliche Einfachheit erkauft war: Für die Herstellung seiner Abzüge investierte er oftmals Wochen. Ob es sich um Aktfotografie, Landschaften, Gefieder, eine Nautilus-Muschel, Sanddünen oder Gemüse handelt, er ging dem Wesen des Motivs mit so unerbittlicher Besessenheit auf den Grund, dass sich dem Betrachter die Beschaffenheit der Oberflächen sinnlich erschliesst. Wie kaum ein anderer vermochte er, das Abstrakte im Gegenständlichen feinfühlig herauszuarbeiten. Mit seiner zu höchster Kunst entwickelten, objektiven und sachlichen Fotografie hat er die Sehgewohnheiten bis in unsere Zeit verändert und geprägt.

Kontakt und Copyright Bild:
Cole Weston Trust
36224 Hwy One Monterey, CA. 93940 USA
www.edward-weston.com

Konrad Wothe

Konrad Wothe (geboren 1952 in München) erhielt seine ersten Einblicke in die Technik der Fotografie bereits mit acht Jahren. Durch einen Optik-Baukasten wurde ihm sozusagen das Handwerk des Mediums von Grund auf vermittelt und so erstaunt es nicht, dass er bis heute selbst gebaute Objektive für seine Arbeit verwendet. Als 18-jähriger gewann er beim Wettbewerb «Jugend forscht» den ersten Preis in Physik für eine selbst kons-

truierte 360-Grad-Panoramakamera. Nach dem Abitur arbeitete er für Heinz Sielmann und beschloss, selbst Tierfilmer und Naturfotograf zu werden. Er studierte an der Universität München Biologie mit Hauptfach Zoologie/Verhaltensforschung sowie Ornithologie. 1982 veröffentlichte Wothe als Coautor mit Prof. Dr. Jürgen Nicolai sein erstes Buch «Fotoatlas der Vögel», 1984 gefolgt vom «Naturführer Vögel». Sein breites fotografisches Repertoire reicht von Tieren, Pflanzen und Landschaften bis hin zur Reisefotografie. Der präzise dokumentarische Stil Konrad Wothes äussert sich besonders deutlich in seinen Arbeiten über Tiere, mit denen er das Ziel verknüpft, Charakter und Verhalten treffend wiederzugeben. Sein 1996 veröffentlichtes Buch «Orang-Utans» zeugt von diesem Bemühen, das Wissenschaftlichkeit und Ästhetik in selten gelungener Form vereint. Diese Fähigkeit fand denn auch weltweite Anerkennung, so konnte Wothe im internationalen Fotowettbewerb der BBC «Wildlife Photographer of the Year» zahlreiche Auszeichnungen entgegennehmen, darunter viermal den ersten und fünfmal den zweiten Preis. 1999 wurde er als GDT-Naturfotograf des Jahres ausgezeichnet und im Fotowettbewerb «Austrian Super Circuit» gewann er 2000 6 Gold-, 1 Silber- und 2 Bronzemedaillen. Konrad Wothe ist Mitglied der Gesellschaft Deutscher Tierfotografen (GDT) und der North American Nature Photography Association.

Kontakt und Copyright Bild:
Konrad Wothe
Kapellenwiese 26, 82377 Penzberg, Deutschland
www.konrad-wothe.de

Günter Ziesler

«Meine Spezialität ist es, nicht spezialisiert zu sein». So umschreibt Günter Ziesler (geboren 1939 in München) den Charakter seiner Passion, der Naturfotografie. Mit 16 Jahren fotografierte er das erste Mal mit der Kamera seines Vaters, einer Voigtländer, Tiere im Münchner Zoo. Schon diese ersten Aufnahmen waren den Motiven gewidmet, die ihn zeitlebens fesseln sollten. Dieses Interesse an der Natur ist Günter Ziesler wohl in die Wiege gelegt. Doch erst mit 34 machte er sein Hobby zum Beruf und schliesslich erhielt er 1977 von einem spanischen Verlag den Auftrag, Aufnahmen für mehrere Bildbände über die Nationalparks südamerikanischer Länder zu machen. 1980 lernte er seine Mitarbeiterin und Ehefrau Angelika Hofer kennen, mit der er 1984 das Buch «Safari» veröffentlichte, Ergebnis einer einjährigen Reise durch Kenia. In einer Auflage von 140 000 Exemplaren in sechs Sprachen erschienen, handelt es sich wohl um

einen der bekanntesten Bildbände zu den Naturwundern Afrikas. Seine besondere Passion galt jedoch stets Südamerika, das er bevorzugt im Campingbus durchstreift. Dabei hat es Ziesler der tropische Regenwald, das schwierigste Gebiet für den Fotografen, besonders angetan. Seine von Bengt Berg und skandinavischen Fotografen wie Hanu Hautula beeinflussten Arbeiten bewegen sich im Spannungsfeld zwischen dynamischen Abläufen und Stillleben, wobei es ihm meisterlich gelingt, allen Bildern eine ikonografische Qualität zu verleihen. So erhält ein Löwenpärchen in seinen Fotografien den Status eines Stilllebens und ein Ausschnitt des Regenwalds die dynamische Ausstrahlung eines Bewegungsablaufs. Die Erhaltung der Umwelt ist Ziesler naturgemäss ein besonderes Anliegen. Seit dem Jahr 2000 wandert die Ausstellung «Abenteuer Regenwald», welche er zusammen mit Angelika Hofer konzipiert hat, zu Schulen und Bibliotheken, um auf die fortschreitende Zerstörung des Regenwaldes aufmerksam zu machen. Bedeutende Publikationen von Ziesler sind unter anderem das 1987 erschienene Buch «Ein Gänsesommer», das ein Jahr darauf herausgekommene «Löwenkinderbuch», 1991 «Urwaldpfade» mit Schilderungen aus dem südamerikanischen Regenwald sowie 1998 «Mahale – Begegnung mit Schimpansen». Das neueste, 2007 erschienene Werk trägt den Titel «Pantanal – Das Herz Südamerikas».

Kontakt und Copyright Bild:
Günter Ziesler
Am Riesenanger 7, 87629 Füssen, Deutschland
www.pan-photography.de

Ulrich Ackermann

Ulrich Ackermann (born 1974) originally completed a photographic apprenticeship at the Hugo Frutig studio in Bern, Switzerland. A specialist in large-scale panoramic images, he prefers to photograph landscapes, nature and travels, but also animals and humans. He finds these not only on his numerous travels, but also at his home. The result of these activities are the influences of aerial photographers such as Georg Gerster and Fred Mayer to the extent that aerial photography, which he adopted after a trip to Alaska, became one of his most important areas of expertise.

Ulrich Ackermann developed the skill to photograph free-hand out of airplanes. In general, he uses analog equipment for his pictures, which he states: "allows for a much more deliberate photography". His spectacular, documentary pictures show a considerable sense of dramatics and staging. It is thus not surprising that for years he dreamed about photographing an entire mountain in one shot, which, in the meantime has become possible with his Hasselblad X-Pan (size 24–65 cm). With this camera, he developed his current area of expertise: a novel, panel format perception not only allows to document landscapes, mountain and water worlds from the air, but also trees and ravines from the hiker's perspective. These panel format photographs convey an unfamiliar image with large and spacious effects. As a young man, Ulrich Ackermann attended free lectures in painting and drawing at the art and trade school in Bern, hence his feeling for painting positively influences his photography in a surprising manner. In this way, the images are unmistakably his in every respect, which he says in his own words "role models are good and motivating, but in the final analysis, one should follow his own feeling for pictures and simply follow through with it, ignoring criticism, in order to find his own photographic handwriting". This handwriting can clearly be seen in Ackermann's photographs of trees with which he contrives to open his fellow man's eyes to the beauty of nature and to appeal to the responsibility to treat it sensibly and with care.

Ackermann has published numerous picture books, among them on places like Alaska, St. Petersburg, Tanzania and the canton of Greyere in Switzerland as well as animal studies on brown bears and swans. His photographs of Greyere were conceived in cooperation with Ilford Imaging and shown at a widely noticed exhibition. His newest book featuring the Val de Trient in the canton of Lower Valais (connection Martigny-Chamonix), with numerous aerial photographs, marks a further milestone of his production which is available at book stores since the beginning of May of this year.

Contact and Copyright Image:
Ulrich Ackermann
Postfach 119, 3000 Bern 7, Switzerland
www.fotolangformat.ch

Ansel Adams

Ansel Easton Adams was born in San Francisco, Calif. on February 20, 1902. After rather difficult early school days, Adams left the regimentations of regular education at the age of twelve in order to continue his education autodidactically. A family trip to Yosemite National Park in 1916 left deep impressions on him which he tried to conserve in the then usual picturesque style of the time. In 1919, his enthusiasm for nature led him to join the Sierra Club dedicated to the environment where he eventually became a member of the board of directors from 1934 until 1971.

Initially, his aim in life was to become a concert pianist and for this he bought a grand piano in 1925. However, shortly after that he saw some photographs by Paul Strand which impressed him so much that he intensified his interest in photography. For some time after, Adams was torn between his desire to become a musician or to make a career as a photographer. In 1930, he met Paul Strand personally, whose precise ideas about good photography led him in 1932 to syndicate the group f/64 with Edward Weston, Imogen Cunningham, John Paul Edwards, Sonya Noskowiak, Henry Swift and Willard van Dyke. The coining of the name for the group originates from the smallest camera aperture allowing for a consistent depth of field from the foreground to the background of the photograph with a maximum exactness to detail in order to capture the group's ideal.

His numerous trips to the Yosemite include some first mountain ascents from which unique documents of nature untouched by the human hand resulted. In 1937, a studio fire destroyed thousands of negatives of the early works of Adams. Towards the end of 1930, he developed his famous "zone system" which has since been used as the most rigorous technique for specifying optimal film exposure in black and white photography. The zone system provides photographers with a systematic method of precisely defining the relationship between the way they see the photographic subject and the results they achieve in their finished works. It allows for a direct correlation between the visual world and the final photographic print. In this way technically perfect negatives are produced that can be enlarged at will. Owing to this system, Adams was able to manipulate the tonal values and to drastically change the emphasis of the motive within the image. A result of his obsession with the techniques of photography was a first textbook "Making a Photograph" published in 1935. "The Basic Photo Series", published in 1948–1956 released the photographic work from the experimental context to allow the layman for the first time, owing to a clear job instruction, to produce consistently outstanding photographic prints. In 1940, Adams conducted the first of the later famous "Yosemite workshops" as well as the "U.S. Camera Photographic Forum" with Edward Weston. In 1952, he helped found the journal "Aperture" and in the year 1958, the already third "Guggenheim Grant", to document the national parks of the USA was bestowed upon him. Many remarkable color pictures are thanks to Adams' acquaintance and collaboration with Edwin Land, the inventor of the instant film technique "Polaroid". In 1963, Adams, together with Nancy Newhall, were given the job to document photographically the University of California. This work titled "Fiat Lux" is among his most famous. Come 1966 he was appointed fellow of the "American Academy of Arts and Sciences", and in 1980 he was bestowed the "Freedom Medal", the highest civil distinction of the United States of America, by President Jimmy Carter.

Ansel Adams died on April 22, 1984 in Carmel, Calif. He left behind his wife Virginia and his two children Michael and Anne. In his memory "The Minarets Wilderness" in the Inyo National Forest were renamed the "Ansel Adams Wilderness". On the first anniversary of his death "Mount Ansel Adams", situated on the southeast boundary of Yosemite National Park, was officially named in his honour.

As hardly another, Ansel Adams, has moulded the photographic heritage of the American west. A whole generation of photographers built upon his work and found stimulation in his overwhelming technical brilliance as opposed to his deep love for nature. Adams was able to express common scenery with illuminating power and intensity, which especially instils nature with an almost religious expressiveness and in this way is able to accentuate aspects of environmental protection.

Contact and Copyright Images:
The Ansel Adams Gallery
P.O. Box 4185, Burlingane, CA 940111, USA
www.anseladams.com

Urs Martin Bachmann

Even as a small child, Urs Bachmann (born 1961) was passionately interested in nature. Already then, he would spend most of his time outdoors in the woods. With his father, who photographed with and old Voigtländer camera, he roamed through the then still largely intact landscapes around Basel. Not far from Muttenz where he then lived, he came across many animals that are rarely seen today; he describes an encounter with an eagle owl and a wood grouse as magical moments in his childhood. Slowly, but surely this close relationship with nature inspired his desire to record his impressions and the way he perceived things with a camera. At the age of 17, he did this while on an Interrail trip through Europe. Shortly after that a world trip took him to Thailand, Malaysia, Bali, Australia, New Zealand and the South Seas, enabling him to record in pictures not only landscapes, fauna and flora, but also new cultures.

After seven years of intensive involvement with photography his first international publication appeared in the renowned magazine "Animan". In the same year a multi-vision slide show followed and by 1997, Urs Bachmann was able to publish his first illustrated book "Faszination Neuseeland" (Fascination New Zealand). While he was influenced by the works of David Muench, Frans Lanting, Jim Brandenburg or Ansel Adams, his own and original current work rather resembles his preoccupation and spiritual relationship with Caspar David Friedrich. Accordingly, Bachmann prefers to photograph at extreme times of the day, either very early in the morning or at dusk, with long exposure times which accentuates the shape of the landscape. With this and other techniques he seeks to retain that special emotional and sensual moment when one feels at one with nature. Here Bachmann's credo is reflected that man as a part of nature must strive to achieve a balance with his environment in order to survive. His newest book, dedicated to probably the most beautiful garden landscapes of the world, Tuscany, is tentatively scheduled to appear in the spring of 2008.

Contact and Copyright Image:
Urs Bachmann
Breitweg 1, 4152 Gempen, Switzerland
www.bachmannurs.ch

Cornelia Dörr

Cornelia Dörr was born in 1963 in Chemnitz, Germany. In 1991, she travelled to Costa Rica where she tried to capture her impressions of the country using a singlelens reflex camera. The difficulty to photograph under the extreme light conditions of the rain forest intensified her interest in photography. She was especially influenced by the works of Scandinavian and American photographers such as Hans Strand, Jan Töve Johansson, Art Wolfe or David Muench. At the moment, she prefers to work with a Nikon D2x, as well as a Hasselblad panorama camera. Cornelia Dörr's dramatically composed images excel through a special variety in the applied elements of design. Her masterly control of superimposed and complementing elements such as intentional blurs, bad weather, abstractions and special light moods creates perfect and expressive portrayals which sharply highlight the beauty of her motives. At the beginning of 1998 she undertook four trips to Patagonia and the Andes. The impressive images of the Patagonian and the Andean landscapes, scarred by wind and ice as well as the sparse plateaus of the Andes, brought Cornelia Dörr and her husband Ramon, who is also a passionate photographer, wide international recognition – in 2000 the BG Wildlife Photographer of the Year Award, 2001 Nature's Best Magazine Award, 2002 first rank in the European competition of nature photography as well as the Gerald Duress Award in 2004. In 2004, an illustrated book with works of Patagonia was especially honoured in the Photographers Hall of Fame with a panoramic photograph of the Grey Glacier (taken in the Chilean National Park, Torres del Paine).

Cornelia Dörr's special personal concern is to open the doors to the public to help them appreciate the fascinations of nature in order to arouse enthusiasm and wonderment and win favour and commitment for the preservation and protection for the "marvels of nature". Cornelia Dörr lives and works in Düsseldorf as a freelance design photographer.

Contact and Copyright Images:
Cornelia Dörr
Eisenstruckstr. 5a, 9114 Chemniz, Germany
www.doerr-naturbilder.de

Heinrich Gohl

At the early age of eight, Heinrich Gohl (born 1926), took his first nature pictures in the garden of his parents' house – an experience that affected him as much as his Sunday walks in the woods with his father. Much later, he became fascinated by nature photography which gave him the vocation to make a career out of photography. After finishing his training as an interior decorator he felt a longing to travel far away from home and first took off to Africa for a year. Under the impressions of an extended sojourn in Alaska, he finally and definitely decided on fully taking up photography as his profession. In 1967, Gohl's first illustrated book "Ein Tag in der Steppe" (A Day in the Steppes) was published to be followed by 25 additional publications which were also translated into 9 languages.

Even if one could see that his early photographs were often influenced by role models like Ansel Adams or Ernst Haas, his first work still features a completely personal natured emotionality which like a red thread of an artistic DNA is shown in all his works. Heinrich Gohl himself explains the outflow as well as the cause of this self-reliance with his love for the matter: "To be sure, for as long as I can remember, I have kept this early acquired affection (for the forest) and this combined sensibility prohibits any callousness on my part". One may well speak of a certain obsession that fuels Heinrich Gohl's activities. It is thus not surprising that he finds vital artistic influence by other obsessed creative artists such as Caspar David Friedrich, Jasper Johns, Ludwig van Beethoven or George Gershwin. None of these were in need of outwardly distinctive artistic features to achieve their own sense of reidentification. The polarization was anyhow a product of their personality and any formalism would have compulsively and artificially limited the scope of their development. Heinrich Gohl is no exception here. Even though his pictures have an unmistakeable signature, they do not come about by a defined angle of view, defined techniques or any other artistically distinguishing marks. It is much more the stance of the photographer that is atmospherically transmitted to the viewers. With his increasing maturity, the sublimation of the atmospherically captured singular instant has increased. In this way, the chosen sections in his newer works are no longer significant for the impact of the pictures. With this, he succeeds brilliantly without resorting to ingratiating photogenic methods to convey his message, focussing his view on the special in the so-called ordinary. As initiator and designer of the exhibition "Forests of the World", Heinrich Gohl's perseverance and verve over the last decade have enabled him to fulfil his long-cherished dream and make it come true. At the same time, a sublimation of his life's work is expressed therein, which, with this intensive mediation of the power and shapes of trees and forests, finds further concentration.

Contact and Copyright Images:
Heinrich Gohl
Arabienstrasse 5, 4059 Basel, Switzerland
www.wald-klima-umwelt.ch

Ernst Haas

Ernst Haas was born on March 2, 1921 in Vienna, Austria. The multi-talented young man applied himself to painting, acting and film, but at first began to study medicine which he stopped in 1947. His great interest in photography let him to trade in food for a camera shortly after the Second World War in spite of his own gnawing hunger! Wanting to master his new piece of equipment, he signed up for a course at the Graphic Arts Institute in Vienna but was rejected at the beginning for his "inactiveness". He found his calling when the editor of the journal "Der Film" advised him against photographing idyllic landscapes but to photograph daily events occurring in wartorn Europe. In 1946, his first deliberately intentional reportage about feeding the poor was printed which was noticed by the publishers of the journal "Heute". "Heute" was the organ of the American occupation and from then on Haas was able to work for both journals as a freelance photojournalist. His photographic recordings of prisoners of war from Russia finally brought him his international breakthrough. The impressive and harrowing pictures were not only published by "Heute", but were also used by the International Red Cross in their efforts to reunite families.
Subsequently, a large portion of the reportage was published by "Life" magazine which resulted in Haas being called upon by the founders of the photo agency "Magnum" to join their circle. In 1950, he became a full member of "Magnum", in 1958 vice president and by 1960 he was president of the agency. By virtue of his intensive experiments with the novel Kodachrome colour film material, at the beginning of 1950 he was commissioned by "Life" magazine to produce a photographic documentary of life in New York. The series published in 1953 was a sensation

and he continued his career with reportages like "The Magic Colours in Motion". This pioneer sports reportage contained heretofore never seen effects like blurred movements and superimposed films. Numerous reportages of cities followed and in 1962, the Museum of Modern Art organized a widely noticed single exhibition of Haas' works. Among numerous book projects his movie "The Art of Seeing" was shown in the 1960s, documented by a touring exhibition sponsored by Kodak. A later television series hosted by him was named after the film. In 1964, a whole range of photographs for John Huston's movie "The Bible" was created. Some of the most outstanding pictures were published by Haas in 1971 in the illustrated book "The Creation". Film and audiovisual techniques were to become some of his lifelong hobbies. Still, he was partial to landscape photography and it is not commonly known that he was responsible for the grandiose and seminal photographs for the "Marlboro" advertising campaign. In the 1970s flowers became increasingly central to Haas' motive, and the multimedia "Flower Show" in 1983 was the highlight of his later work.
Shortly before his death in New York on September 12, 1986, he was honoured with the Hasselblad Award. Haas' special place in the history of photography manifests itself from his experimental handling of colour photography where he achieved groundbreaking results. His sensational, flickering style of colour photographs increasingly changed in the 1970s to the more sedate and more precise expression shown especially in his books on Zen-Buddhism (Himalayan Pilgrimage, 1978). His inartificial ethical approach to photography is especially made clear by his own powerful expressions: "I'm not interested in photographing new motives – I would like to see things in a new way". "With photography a new language has been created. For the first time, it is now possible to express reality with reality." "My theory of composition? Very simple: only press the shutter when everything in the viewfinder is in its right place!". His direct and forthright views are also expressed in that Haas did not think much of the marketing dogma cultured by many of his colleagues. "The camera does not make the difference. Everybody takes in what one sees. But one must simply see it!"

Contact and Copyright Images:
Estate of Ernst Haas
c/o Silverstein Photography
535 West 24th Street
New York, NY 10011 USA
www.ernst-haas.com

Mike Hill

Mike Hill, born 1949 in England, originally used photography only to document his interest in Natural History. Equipped with a Zenith Photosniper outfit, he took black and white photographs of birds. Even though these early experiments did not match his expectations, he gradually began to experiment with interpretations of the natural world rather than purely recording it. Influenced by Ernst Haas and Jim Brandenburg, he developed a signature combination of shutter speed and compositional techniques which result in dramatic images allowing a very direct and emotional approach to nature. The spirit of places and the character of animals become vibrantly alive for the viewer and attention is drawn to details which would escape untrained eyes without the help of the amplifying forces of the photographer's alert eye. Hill claims to be influenced by music and painting, this becomes evident in his carefully composed images which truly are "painted by light". Among his most notable achievements are six photographic books on the natural world, especially well known are those on the nature of the Arabian Gulf and the Middle East. His lifelong quest for the beauty in the natural world has earned him 14 awards in the Wildlife Photographer of the Year competition. He uses both a 35mm and a 6x17cm panoramic camera and prefers to work with digital equipment. One of Hills main driving forces is his great interest in the conservation of the natural world. This not only shows itself in the fact that his work was very important in changing the attitude of governments and citizens towards the wildlife in the Middle East. It is also very much evident in his latest project which involves photographic interpretations of the special atmosphere of Dartmoor in Britain.

Contact and Copyright Image:
Mike Hill
The White Trillium, Stevenstone, Torrigton
Devon EX38 7HY, Great Britan
www.mikehillimages.com

Eberhard Hummel

Eberhard Hummel (born 1939), is one of Europe's most distinguished nature photographers. His photographic career began when he secretly photographed his teachers while attending school classes. His love for nature is reflected in his efforts to achieve an unaltered detailed reproduction of the subject he has chosen for his photographs. Sojourns in North Africa, South America and the Antarctic as well as extended trips to the Sahara left their mark on his work, which was also influenced by the American photographer David Muench. Regular contributions to illustrated books, calendars and various periodicals show just how much empathy Hummel has for the different shapes and characteristic in his landscapes. This is also true for his animal portraits which are distinguishable through their extraordinary directness and immediacy.

Eberhard Hummel understands how to catch the special moment the way it presents itself to the viewer without being dramatic. His ability to reflect the beauty of nature in an unaffected manner is his contribution, to the protection and preservation of nature by animating the public to take action to ensure that the beauty is not destroyed.

Contact and Copyright Image:
Eberhard Hummel
Rüderer Strasse 13, 73733 Esslingen, Germany
www.naturbilder.de/EberhardHummel/

Frans Lanting

Frans Lanting, born in 1951 in Rotterdam, belongs to the outstanding nature photographers of our time. His influential photographs appear in books, periodicals and exhibitions worldwide. For more than two decades he has been documenting our relationship with nature in various environments, reaching from the Amazon to the Antarctic. He portrays animals as goodwill ambassadors for the conservation of whole ecosystems and his publications play a large role in sharpening the awareness of endangered ecological treasures. Lanting regularly works for the National Geographic Society. For their magazine, he not only searched for the legendary Bonobos of central Africa, but also sailed around South Georgia in a spectacular publicity campaign. Lanting's newest works treat especially important ecological and sensitive areas of the world not only for instance the volcanoes of Hawaii, but also the Luangwa Valley in Zambia. His books have received many prizes and honours: "nobody is able to transform animals into art better than Frans Lanting" writes for instance "The New Yorker". Classic examples of nature photography can be found among his most important publications: Jungles (2000), Penguin (1999), Living Planet (1999), Eye to Eye (1997), Bonobo, The Forgotten Ape (1997), Okavango: Africa's last Eden (1993), Forgotten Edens (1993) and Madagascar, A World Out of Time (1990).

During the last few years Lanting has been working all over the world with different scientists such as palaeobiologists and astrophysicists in order to publish his newest project "Life, A Journey Through Time". This project deals with his personal interpretation of the evolution of the earth. Frans Lanting has been bestowed numerous prominent honours for his dedicated work. In 2001, he was bestowed the title "Knight of the Golden Ark" by his Royal Highness, Prince Bernhard, the highest decoration for environmental protection in the Netherlands. World Press Photo has also honoured Frans Lanting on various occasions; furthermore, he held the title of the "BBC Wildlife Photographer of the Year" and the Sierra Club accorded him the "Ansel Adams Award". In 1999, the London Royal Photographic Society admitted him into their ranks. In addition, he is member of the founding panel of the "University of California" in Santa Cruz, Calif. and the National Council of the World Wildlife Fund (WWF) where he has a regular column "The Outdoor Photographer". Frans Lanting lives and works closely with his wife Christina Eckstrom in Santa Cruz, Calif.

Contact and Copyright Images:
Frans Lanting Photography
207 McPherson Street, Suite D
Santa Cruz, CA 95060 USA
www.lanting.com

Christian Lichtenberg

Christian Lichtenberg was born in Basel in 1953. Extensive travel took him to countries like Japan, the USA, Africa and Brazil. Next to numerous other awards, he received the Grand Prize of the Biennial Festival in São Paolo, Brazil. "Zen or the art of squeezing the trigger", this is the way Christian Lichtenberg circumscribes the developing process of his art, the much reduced, internalized images that are not only prospects and views, but also communicate deeper insight. The "painting with light" directs him far into the age old atavistic questions of humanity about sense and purpose, which cannot be answered because man has no finer instrument for contemplation at his disposal than his own brain.

For twenty years, using black and white photography, Lichtenberg explored ways of thinking through which he could communicate iconographic picture compositions which he subjectively drew from the collective subconscious. This phase culminated in the exhibition "My Private Universe" eventually to be replaced by a less anecdotic tinctured picture language which increasingly used colour photography. Lichtenberg utilized this development to approach the character of nature, the recognisability of the motive remaining secondary. In spite of his combined reflection of the inner and outer world, Lichtenberg's personality continues to be present in "squeezing the trigger". His pictures are coined by a self-evident creative will the stringency of which unlocks it to the viewer who is engaged with the picture. In this way, the special adapted ties in identification with the motive may well be the reason that Christian Lichtenberg is able to touch and move humanity.

Contact and Copyright Image:
Christian Lichtenberg
Schanzenstr. 46, 4056 Basel, Switzerland
www.lichtenberg.ch

Patrick Loertscher

Patrick Loertscher (born 1964 in Bern) is one of the most successful and innovative nature photographers in Europe. His interest in photography was sparked early by photographic features in magazines like National Geographic, Geo or Merian. But he was also fascinated by the fashion photography he saw in periodicals such as Vogue and Vanity Fair. He decided to become a photographer when he was still at grammar school. After a voluntary traineeship at the Swiss publishing house Ringier, he started an apprenticeship as photo-lithographer at the art and trade school in Bern. Already then and later as an employee as a photo-lithographer, he undertook many trips to Asia, Australia and New Zealand on which he ventured to tap the genre of landscape photography. In 1994, Patrick Loertscher set up his own publishing house which he recently complemented with the Patrick Loertscher Wilderness Gallery in Heiden in Canton Appenzell, Switzerland. His broad technical skills allow him to produce very large format photographs. On the basis of his occupation, it is not surprising that he prefers to use the analogous technique. Loertscher's dramatically staged pictures testify his search for unique moods that drastically differ from the postcard serenity of sedate fair-weather images. He is obviously influenced by the powerful colour works of Art Wolfes and, in combination with Loertscher's intuition for the forms of the photographed landscape impressions, his work portrays an especially harmonious symbiosis. His ability to precisely fathom the characters of diverse areas of unspoiled nature may well stem from the knowledgeable depth of his motives. This also explains his passion to pass impressions from the wilderness on to other people. Next to his numerous calendars Patrick Loertscher has also published two major illustrated books about the nature wonders of Europe and New Zealand.

Contact and Copyright Images:
Patrick Loertscher
Quellenweg 3, 9410 Heiden, Switzerland
www.patrickloertscher.com

Graeme Matthews

Graeme Matthews was born in 1949 in Blenheim, New Zealand. His interest in photography was triggered by finding a disused Kodak Brownie box camera in a cupboard of his parents home. Taking it with him on long bicycle trips to the countryside he gathered his first experiences in photography with it. In 1983 his first major publication "The Edge of the Land" – a book on the coastline of New Zealand – was published. Graeme Matthews' work is influenced by Ansel Adams and he also claims that "The Creation", a book by Ernst Haas played an important role for him. Apart from that, music ranging from classical to jazz, blues and country is a major artistical influence in his life. His love of nature led to his most notable commission, which involved photographing trees in more than 44 countries for a book project. This exemplary project fits perfectly to what Graeme Matthews himself describes as the lifelong quest in his photography: "to show the beauty of nature and impress upon people the need to look after it." Unlike most contemporary photographers he does not use digital technology but a wide variety of different traditional cameras, underlining his documenting rather than designing style. Together with his wife Jenny with whom he works in a team, Graeme Matthews lives and works on the sea-coast of New Zealand, one of the world's important scenic places and as such a major inspiration to his work as well.

Contact and Copyright Images:
Graeme R. Matthews
Rarangi, R.D. 3, Blenheim New Zealand
www.graeme-matthews.com

Klaus Nigge

Klaus Nigge (born 1956) originally utilized photography to document his observations in the animal kingdom. He studied philosophy, art and biology, a specialist area which later on deepened his knowledge on focussing on botany/plant sociology. At about the age of 28, it increasingly occurred to him that through experience and observation the impact and intensity of his subjects could be increased through the deployment of photography. In 1994, Klaus Nigge became a self-employed photographer. In 1997, he published his first book "Kamtschatka. Adler, Bären und Vulkane" (Kamchatka. Eagles, Bears and Volcanoes). By 1999, National Geographic published an article on giant white-tailed eagles which started a lasting cooperation with this journal of renown for Klaus Nigge. In the same year, another book was published that was also dedicated to eagles and in 2004 he published "Die Rückkehr des Königs: Wisente in Polens Urwäldern" (The Return of the King: Wisents (European bisons) in the Primeval Forests of Poland). Furthermore, Klaus Nigge regularly contributes to periodicals such as Geo, Terre Sauvage and Arione. In addition, he has been bestowed numerous prizes such as the "Gerald Durell Award" or the "Wildlife Photographer of the Year". At first sight Nigge's pictures appear pleasantly calm, they radiate a quality of deep inner tranquillity. Only at second sight does it become clear just how carefully he traces the characters of the depicted animals and their surroundings. It is not surprising that images from Hannu Hautalas, Frans Lanting, Michio Hoschinos or Michael Nichols had a lasting effect on him. Capturing the atmosphere is of central importance: "to photograph hidden emotions such as sounds and scents, respectively to suggest them, belongs to one of the most exciting challenges". This is the way he also sees analogies in portrait photography, where it is less important to produce colourful pictures, but rather to refine the personality of the subject, a process that is decisive for him in nature photography. Klaus Nigge's enthusiasm for the straight, the true and the genuine allies perfectly with his profound knowledge of biology, art and philosophy. Neither the compulsive natural nor the obtrusive artificiality in his pictures outweigh this balance in his works. He offers the public the chance to sit down and give consideration to the importance of animals and landscapes, the environment and finally the earth.

Contact and Copyright Images:
Klaus Nigge
Ernst-Becker-Strasse 12, 44534 Lünen, Germany
klaus.nigge@t-online.de

Beat Presser

Rare are the photographers who were able to make it on the international scene. To take the leap without making great compromises is nearly impossible. Beat Presser (born in Basel 1952) has been successful in being able to pursue his personal interests, to afford his projects the necessary gestation and to preserve a wide view of the photographer's profession without falling into the trap of specialising or limiting himself to a defined motive. The versatility of his work proves it: it can be seen that somebody who does not have to resort to monotone superficialities in order to be distinctive is at work here. He cannot be categorized and certainly plays in a league of his own. Still his image compositions display specific characteristics.

The tension in Presser's pictures has a property that often results from a confrontation which may not only be because of the motive, but also the exposure technique. On the other hand, his work draws a continuous line of interest on the power of abstraction; although this is not an abstraction from the superficially rakish appearance that ultimately results from a flat emptiness. Presser's abstraction highlights, accentuates correlations and produces rich and copious image compositions which can be overpowering, but more often than not appear introspective. At this point, it becomes evident that the most important goal of the seasoned globe trotter is the mediation of impressions made under most difficult conditions, because these impressions lead to him – Presser's photographs are testimony of this most difficult trip of all. Still this in not the only way he allows the spectator to take part in his journey. Next to being visiting Professor in Europe, Africa, South America and Asia, he also organises exhibitions and is especially concerned with the photographic education of children and adolescents.

In view of the autonomy of Presser's perspectives, it becomes evident that he was searching for his very own personal approach to photography. As early as the age of seven, he began taking photographs; his first picture depicting a garden gnome next to a daffodil is still preserved. At the age of 15, he first observed how a photograph actually emerges from film in the developing bath. This event signalled his determination to become a photographer. At the beginning of the 1970s, he was able to work with fashion photographers Onorio Mansutti in Basel as well as with Just Jaeckin in Paris. During his time in Paris he made intensive use of the Cinémathèque de France that opened the world of the moving picture. Paris, too, is where he first saw the movie "Aguirre, the Wrath of God" and made contact with the work of Werner Herzog and Klaus Kinski which awakened a desire in him to work with these giants of the film industry. Back in Basel, during the middle of the 1970s, he began to educate himself as a cameraman and for two years, starting in 1976, he published his own photographic journal "The Village Cry", which proved to be way ahead of its time. The edition 4/1977 contains a reportage on Klaus Kinski and Daniel Schmid. Werner Herzog hired Beat Presser in 1981 as still photographer and camera assistant for "Fitzgeraldo" and in 1987 for "Cobra Verde". Within the framework of these projects, the world famous portraits of Klaus Kinski resulted. During the following years Beat Presser created numerous documentary and cultural films. Since 1988, he has worked together with Vera Pechel in Madagascar on a documentary film and on the photographic project "Vom Feuer zur Religion" (From Fire to Religion). The series "Baobab" shown at the exhibition originated in this connection. In 1998, he published his book "Alpentraum", a debate with his homeland. After this, he began to devote himself intensively with Buddhism. Starting in Thailand, he worked for 5 years in the monasteries of India, Myanmar, Laos, Sri Lanka and Cambodia. As a result of this, the book "Oase der Stille" (Oasis of Silence) was published in 2005, marking for the present the highlight of Beat Presser's efforts to atmospherically communicate his search for truth and authenticity.

Contact and Copyright Images:
Beat Presser
P.O. Box 1845, 4001 Basel, Switzerland
www.beatpresser.com

Albert Renger-Patzsch

Albert Renger-Patzsch was born in Würzburg, Germany in 1897. His father Robert Renger-Patzsch was an enthusiastic amateur photographer himself and became famous for his technical innovations. As early as at the age of 14, Albert was able to master numerous photographic techniques and as he recalls: "at the age of 14, I already knew all there was to know about offset printing and began photographing in all formats with my father's apparatuses, although without his knowledge."
In the First World War, Albert Renger-Patzsch qualified for an assignment in a chemical central office of the general staff. In 1919, he began to study chemistry, only to terminate it in 1921 as he was given the opportunity to assume responsibility for the picture archives of Folkwang Publishers in Hagen. Ernst Fuhrmann, manager of Folkwang and Auriga Publishers, recognized Renger-Patzsch's talents and suggested to undertake the publication of his first works "Orchids" and "Crassula". In 1923, he changed location to move to Kronstadt, Romania where he had

work as a press agent for pictures and shortly after as a bookseller in a drugstore. Fuhrmann soon convinced him to return to Hagen. Finally, as of 1925 Renger-Patzsch worked as a self-employed photographer and published his book "Das Chorgestühl von Cappenberg" (The Choir Stalls of Cappenberg). His breakthrough came with the book "Die Welt ist Schön" (The World Is Beautiful), published in 1928, which was to become one of the basics of modern photography, helping the "Neuen Sachlichkeit" (The New Objectivity) in Germany to succeed. Albert Renger-Patzsch's ability to emphasise the aesthetics and beauty in the industrial motive, brought about many assignments from industry, architecture and commercial areas. In 1929, he was allocated studio facilities at the Folkwang museum in Essen to assume professorship as tutor of the special department "Bildmässige Fotografie" (Pictorial Photography) at the Folkwang school. He left that post after two terms because of differences with the national socialists. In 1944, his studio was destroyed by a bomb attack, which also lay waste his photo archive. Following this, he resettled with his family to Wamel at the Möhnsee, Germany. Even though he realized many assignments from the industry, his focus of attention increasingly changed to nature photography. His later publications were the illustrated book "Landschaft zwischen Ruhr und Möhne" (Landscape between Ruhr and Möhne) in 1957, "Bäume" (Trees) in 1962 and "Gestein" (Rocks) in 1966, the same year that Albert Renger-Patzsch died.
His artistic legacy in its innovative importance for photography cannot be overestimated. Renger-Patzsch above all others was one of the first photographers to realize and visually render the aesthetics of industrial installations and products. On this basis, he caused a still continuing change of paradigm, since most of his motives were regarded as unworthy by his contemporaries. At the same time he emancipated photography from the artistic style of painting. Up until "The New Objectivity", photography was regarded as an inferior substitute for painting, whereof the techniques of the painted pictures are proof of imitating pictorialism. True to his motto: "let us leave art to the artists and try to create by means of photography photographs that are able to persist by their photographic qualities", Renger-Patzsch piloted the inner qualities to a completely new direction to find, in this way, areas of motives that were otherwise not adequately presentable. As he said himself: "to measure up in grasping in pictures the rigidly ordered structures of lines in modern technique, the airy grating of the cranes and bridges, the dynamics

of machines of 1,000 horsepower, is probably only possible through photography." Also, his late tree photographs always demonstrate his unmistakable eye for structures and surfaces. Renger-Patzsch considered contrast as too superficial a means to achieve tension and effects. Much more so, he sounded out delicate arches of tension between structure and surface. This leads to perfect, in themselves restful pictures that are still free of contemplative boredom, since dramaturgy and light air float by visually subliminal ever more powerful into consciousness. In 1957, the Gesellschaft für Deutsche Lichtbildner (Society of German Photographers) accorded him their David Octavius Hill Medal, the Biennale in Venice honoured him with the gold medal. The Deutsche Gesellschaft für Fotografie (German Society for Photography) decorated him in 1960 with the Prize for Culture. In 1961, he was awarded the gold medal of the Fotografische Gesellschaft Wien (Photographic Society of Vienna) and in 1965 the Staatspreis des Kunsthandwerks des Landes Nordrhein-Westfalen (State Prize of the Arts and Trade of the State of North Rhine Westphalia).

Contact and Copyright Images:
Archiv Ann und Jürgen Wilde
Niederberger Strasse 23, 53909 Zülpich, Germany
www.karl-blossfeld-archiv.de

Norbert Rosing

Norbert Rosing was born 1953 in the Muensterland, Germany. When he saw a demonstration of the single lens reflex camera at his elementary school, he was so excited about the creative possibilities he saw that he set up bowling pins to earn some money to buy his first camera. He first started photographing the surroundings of Berchtesgaden, Bavaria, but soon discovered Scandinavia which began his long-term fascination for the Nordic countries. In 1988, Rosing changed over to the Leica R-System to start the project "Im Reich des Polarbären" (In the Realm of the Polar Bear). It soon became evident that with this he had found a motive which he, like no other, was able to put it in the limelight. Rosing feels that: "The Arctic is like a book with a thousand pages that opens itself anew every day". At this point his world-famous photographs of polar bears led him to further interesting projects about national parks in Germany and the USA (Yellowstone). In 1992, Rosing took the risk and became self employed. The versatility of his pictures continue to surprise and his aptitude to transport atmospheres and emotions with his photography especially draws the beholder into their spell. The more so, since he rarely uses special effects, but works with light moods and landscape forms. In this manner, he includes the animal in the landscape of animal photography or looks upon it as a part of it. Rosing is convinced to have found his handwriting by using the Leica R-System. Accordingly, the technical aspect in photography is important for him where he especially appreciates the resulting almost three-dimensionality of the slide, which would otherwise not be possible with a digital technique. His concern for the conservation of authentic nature photography, without needing digital processing also marks his original and natural pictorial language that best subsists without resorting to excessive aesthetics.

Rosing's pictures are published in numerous publications. They appear regularly in Geo as well as in the National Geographic magazine. He has had six illustrated books published, one each of national parks in Germany and Yellowstone, two of Polar Bears, one of cheetahs as well as "Die Nacht ist wie ein stilles Meer" (The Night Is Like a Still Ocean), a poetic sheet of pictures. He is a member of the German Society for Photography, the Society of German Animal Photographers, the North American Nature Photography Association and the International League of Conservation Photographers. Over and above these memberships, he assumes special responsibility for the protection of nature as a consulting member of Polar Bears International.

Contact and Copyright Images:
Norbert Rosing
Amselweg 15, 82284 Grafrath, Germany
www.rosing.de

Hans-Peter Schaub

"Nature is never trivial – always different", this is the way Hans-Peter Schaub (born 1961) describes his personal access to nature photography. He traces his interests in photography back to his art classes in high school during which he took his first pictures. After studying biology and after having received his PhD in 1993, he has been working as a professional photo journalist since 1995. His first book "Der Kaiserstuhl" (The Kaiserstuhl, a region in South Western Germany) was published in 2002. Since then Schaub has published numerous works, among them some illustrated books about the Black Forest as well as a book about the "Pfälzerwald" (Forest in the Palatinate). To some of his role models,

he counts Frans Lanting, Ansel Adams, Shinzo Maeda, Henri Cartier-Bresson, Andreas Feininger and Galen Powell. Already in the introductory citation, Hans-Peter Schaub articulates his claim to comprehend photography as a creative challenge. Schaub's closeness to nature and his atmospherically charged pictures reflect his personal attitude through which he aims to obtain and to express his points of view. In this way, the function of every single picture is for the beholder to reflect on the depicted image and form an opinion about it. A clear social motive is noticeable which is generally valid for the visual arts. It is not surprising that Schaub not only takes his influence from other photographers, but also from music and painting, for instance the works of William Turner, Caspar David Friedrichs, August Mackes and even Paul Cézannes. Because of this broad palette of inspiration he does not feel any fundamental difference between portrait and landscape photography; he also believes that as facial expressions, postures, and glances are ever changing, landscapes, too, are subjected to a continuing process of change. Hans-Peter Schaub gets to the point when he says: "the art with both great topics is to release the trigger at the right moment – whereby there are mostly not only one, but more right moments". With this reliable view for the alternative, Schaub succeeds in sometimes staging well-known motives in a new and unusual manner.

Contact and Copyright Image:
Hans-Peter Schaub
Waldorfweg 41, 59063 Hamm, Germany
www.hanspeterschaub.de

Emil Schulthess

Emil Schulthess was born on October 29, 1913 in Zurich. After an apprenticeship as graphic artist, he became guest student of the photographer Hans Finsler at the Art and Trade School in Zurich. The early 1930s took him to Paris, after which he made a name for himself as a freelance graphic artist. Numerous works in the area of tourism show just how excellent Schulthess was able to deal with the abstract style of the time. In 1937, he married his wife Bruna and became house graphic artist at the Printing and Publishing House Conzett Huber. There the monthly periodical "Du" was published, for which he was responsible for the graphic design and picture editing. In 1950, he undertook the project of a 360° panorama of the sun's orbit on the island Hekkingen in Norway, a topic that occupied him for the rest of his life. From 1951 until 1990,

Schulthess was responsible for the design of the Swiss Calendar. In 1952, he was awarded the "US Camera Award" for his Midnight Sun Panorama. The year after that he took a trip across the USA, which he documented in 1955 with a much recognized illustrated book. For the book "Wildtiere im Kongo" (Wild Animals in the Congo), as well as additional publications about Africa, Schulthess undertook in 1955/56 an adventuresome crossing of the African continent. The American Society of Magazine Photographers honoured him for both these projects in 1958 with their "Annual Award". During the following years he ventured to Japan, Hong-Kong as well as the Philippines which reflected itself in splendid illustrated books capturing the sensuous brilliance of East Asia. Subsequent to these activities, he took part in an expedition to the Antarctic by the US Navy and the National Science Foundation. As early as 1960, the pictures resulting from this were published in the widely recognized book "Antarctica" and introduced in "Life". The years 1960 till 1962 brought about various trips to South America, which led to the book project "Amazonas" (The Amazon).

Various of Schulthess' photographs were also shown at the exhibition "Photography in Fine Arts" at the Metropolitan Museum of Modern Art. Carl Foreman's movie "The Victors" offered Schulthess the possibility to produce portraits of, for instance, Romy Schneider, Jeanne Moreau and George Hamilton. Come 1964, he was bestowed the Culture Prize of the German Society for Photography and in the same year, he left again for a great trip, this time for communist China. In 1966, the corresponding illustrated book was launched, printed in an edition of 50,000 copies, and was received with enormous echo. His works on Africa and China brought him the "US Camera Achievement Award" in 1967. In 1969 and 1970, he accomplished a 360° panorama of the mount Dufour peak, which was initially shown at the world exhibition in Osaka and then published in numerous publications. As a result of his many trips behind the iron curtain, the book "Sowjetunion" (Soviet Union) appeared in 1971. Because of the insight into the communist superpower, the book was regarded a sensation and was a great success right from the beginning. In the year after that the influential travelling exhibition "Unspoiled Nature", which was supported by Kodak, went on tour in many countries. In the 1970s Emil Schulthess increasingly engaged himself with technical difficulties of the panorama technique which he developed to perfection. Between 1974 and 1978, various publications containing his panorama pictures were published and as a result he was commissioned to design the New Year edition for the Asahi newspaper in Tokyo. Such an honour was never before bestowed on a foreigner and Schulthess mastered this difficult task with a 360° panorama of Mount Fuji. In the same year his illustrated book "Swiss Panorama" won the "Goldene Letter" (The Golden Letter) as one of the most beautiful books in the world. In 1984, the then world largest colour enlargement in the dimensions of 82 x 7.2 m, also a Schulthess picture, was produced for the Swiss Pavilion at Expo 85. The book "Landschaft der Urzeiten" (Landscape of Prehistoric Times) published in 1988, was to be his last great publishing project. Emil Schulthess died on January 20, 1996. The uniqueness of his work is a result of his unmistakeable taste of image compositions that unlock ever new aspects even after repeated viewing and so distinguish themselves clearly from the works of other landscape photographers of the time.

With his pictures, Schulthess understood how to capture and delight both the heart and eye of the beholder. As a mediator between the cultures, his publications allowed first and longed for insights into the strange and different. The elegant fashion in which he succeeded is testimony of his love for humanity and the wonders of the earth. In appreciation of his work in the Antarctic, the point 84°74' latitude south and 115°00' longitude west, was officially named the "Schulthess Buttress".

Contact and Copyright Images:
Emil Schulthess Erben, Photoarchiv
Zollikerstrasse 128, CH - 8008 Zurich, Switzerland
www.emil-schulthess.ch

Hans Strand

Hans Strand was born in 1955 and soon after graduating from the Royal Institute of Technology in Stockholm, Sweden in 1981 he began a career in mechanical engineering. However, he decided in 1990 after nine years to devote full-time attention to his hobby and to become a landscape photographer. Always drawn to the untamed and unmanipulated facets of nature, Strand never regretted this change of direction. "The wilderness is the mother of all things. It is always honest and never trivial." Following this remark of himself, he set out from the landscapes of Scandinavia and later took the entire planet as his motif, photographing everything from the vast expanses of the Arctic to steaming rain forests and dry deserts. His work has been published in many internationally acclaimed photography

magazines and he lectures in Sweden and internationally. In 1995 his first book „And the Sea Never Rests" was published, followed by „For as Long as the Forests Grow" in 1998. His photographs were chosen for Canon's international calendar in 1999, in the same year he was awarded the "Nature of the Year" commendation by the Swedish Nature Protection Agency. In 2001 his landscape photographs won in "The European Nature Photographer of the Year" competition. His third book, "The Eighth Day" was published in 2002. The Swedish photo magazine FOTO presented him with the "Nordic Photographer of the Year" distinction in 2003. His latest publication, "Arctic Impressions" will come to bookshops in 2007.

Contact and Copyright Images:
Hans Strand
Hertgvägen 3, 12652 Hägersten, Sweden
www.hansstrand.com

Jan Töve

Jan Töve Johansson was born in Boras, Sweden, in 1958. After he saw his father's black and white photographs, he began to be interested in photography himself. At the age of 12, he won his first camera in a competition. As early as 1975, he was able to profit from his first success by winning a photographic competition sponsored by a hunting magazine.

On multiple occasions, he was elected "BBC Wildlife Photographer of the year"; moreover, in 1995, he was awarded the prize "Nordic Photographer of the Year" by the Swedish journal "Foto". The Swedish administration for environmental protection bestowed upon him the title "Nature Photographer of the Year" in 2003. Since his first book "Speglingar", published in 1996, Jan Töve has edited numerous publications that have been greatly recognized the world over and have won many honours. In 2001, he started working on a documentation project along the Viskan river in Sweden. The photographs resulting from this work show intrinsically the wingspan of the very timely range in Jan Töve's vision. He always sees his motives as landscapes, be they in reference to nature or social events. In his photographs, humans are almost always also depicted by chance in their natural surroundings and by that constitute a part of Jan Töve's landscapes.

It is not so much his concern to emphasise contrasting impressions, but rather to join these contrasts together and embed them in an overall picture. In this way, he shows just how much humans and the products of their civilisation are

an integral part of the landscapes of this earth. Jan Töve Johansson lives and works as a landscape photographer, journalist and author in Sweden, where he also attends to his commitment to train future photographers.

Contact and Copyright Images:
Prästgården, Härna 150
523 99 Hökerum, Sweden
www.jantove.com

Christian Vogt

Christian Vogt was born in 1946 in Basel, Switzerland. Since 1970 he has been designing concepts for himself and, on commission, books, monographs, catalogues and exhibitions.

Contact and Copyright Images:
Studio Christian Vogt
P.O. Box 2226, CH - 4001 Basel, Switzerland
www.christianvogt.com

Edward Weston

Edward Weston was born on March 24, 1886 in Highland Park, Illinois, USA. At an early age he started to be interested in photography and at the age of 16 he was given his first camera; a Kodak Bull's Eye No. 2. His pictures were successful to such a degree that they were exhibited a year after in 1903 at the Art Institute in Chicago, Ill. After this, he worked as an itinerant photographer working his way to California where he settled as a portrait photographer in 1906. Three years later he married his first wife Flora May Chandler, he had four sons with her. By 1911 he was able to open his first photographic studio in Tropico, Calif.; in 1919 he became a member of the London Salon of Photography. During this time Weston renounced the pictorial style of the time which aimed as much as possible to achieve a "painted" and impressionistic impression of the photographed portraits. Weston became thus one of the founders of "straight photography", which dedicated itself to an as realistic as possible rendition of the photographed motive. In 1923, he travelled to Mexico City with his apprentice photographer and lover Tina Modotti, where he operated his own studio, only to return to California after five years to open a studio in Carmel. At that time, he gradually coached his son Brett into photography who supported his father at the studio. In 1932, Weston founded the group f/64 together with Ansel Adams, Willard van Dyke, Imogen Cunningham and others in New York. The coining of the name for the group originates from the smallest camera aperture allowing for a consistent depth of field from the foreground to the background of the photograph with a maximum exactness to detail in order to ideally capture the group's ideal of "straight photography". Accordingly, the manifesto of the group puts forth that photography must consistently be independent of ideological conventions in art or aesthetics. Weston became the first photographer there was to receive a Guggenheim Fellowship in 1937. In 1938, he married his assistant Charis Wilson. The 1930s and 40s were extremely productive years for Weston, thus many picture books were published that were illustrated with his pictures. Among them such important works as Walt Whitman's poems "Leaves of Grass" or the standard work "My Camera on Point Lobos". At that time, the rugged coast of Point Lobos was the experimental field for Weston's first colour pictures which impressively demonstrate his versatility. Instinctively, he developed an equally independent approach to the motive for his colour works as for his black and white ones. He comments on his trials of 1947: "If somebody argues that at some point colour will replace black and white in photography, he is talking nonsense. That is to say that colour and black and white are not competing with one another; we're dealing with different means to achieve various goals." Parallel to these trials, Willard van Dyke started the movie "The Photographer" in which Edward Weston's working method is documented. Unfortunately, because of his deteriorating Parkinson disease, in the same year, he had to give up experimenting with colour. After he got ill, his sons Brett and Cole as well as Brett's wife Dody Warren produced about 800 prints of his most important photographs under his guidance. In recognition of Weston's outstanding position in the American history of photography, he was appointed honorary member of the American Photographic Society. Edward Weston died on January 1, 1958 in Carmel, Calif. Through technical mastery he managed to succeed in creating pictures of unusual structural wealth which guide the beholder to the beauty and finesse of even the simplest objects. Weston's diaries point out at which high price this alleged simplicity was acquired: for the production of his prints he often invested weeks. Regardless if he dealt with centrefolds, landscapes, feathering, a nautilus muscle, sand dunes or vegetables, he explored the character of the motive with unrelenting obsession to sensually open the composition of the surfaces for the observer. As hardly any other, Weston was able to sensitively carve out the abstract in objectivity. With his objective and unpretentious photography he has changed and shaped our seeing habits right up to the present time.

Contact and Copyright Images:
Cole Weston Trust
36224 Hwy One
Monterey, CA. 93940 USA
www.edward-weston.com

Konrad Wothe

Konrad Wothe, born 1952 in Munich, Germany, had first insight into the technique of photography at the early age of eight. An optic construction kit gave him his basic skills and it is thus not surprising that up until today he uses self-constructed objects for his work. At the age of 18, he won first prize in physics at the contest "Jugend forscht" (Youth doing research) for a self-constructed 360° panorama camera. After graduating from high school, he worked for Heinz Sielmann and decided to become an animal and nature photographer himself. He studied biology at the University of Munich and he took zoology/behavioural research and ornithology as his main subjects. In 1982, Wothe published, as co-author to Professor Jürgen Nicolai, his first book titled "Fotoatlas der Vögel" (Illustrated Atlas on Birds), followed in 1984 by "Naturführer Vögel" (Nature Guide Birds). His broad photographic repertoire extends from animals, plants and landscapes to travel photography. The precise documentary style of Konrad Wothe comes especially to the fore in his works about animals, with which he ties in the goal to aptly reflect their character and behaviour. His book "Orang-Utans" published in 1996 is evidence of his desire to combine concepts of science and aesthetics in a rarely successful manner. This ability found him recognition worldwide and thus Wothe was awarded many prizes from the international photo competition of BBC "Wildlife Photographer of the Year", among them four times first prize and five times runner up. In 1999, he was decorated GDT-Nature Photographer of the Year and in the photographic competition "Austrian Super Circuit" in 2000, he won 6 gold, 1 silver and 2 bronze medals. Konrad Wothe is a member of the Society of German Animal Photographers (GDT) and of the North American Nature Association.

Contact and Copyright Images:
Konrad Wothe
Kapellenwiese 26, 82377 Penzberg, Germany
www.konrad-wothe.de

Günter Ziesler

"My specialty is not to be specialized". This is how Günter Ziesler, born 1939 in Munich, Germany, describes the character of his passion, nature photography. At the age of 16, he used his father's, Voigtländer camera for the first time photographing animals at the Munich Zoo. Already at this point, these first photographs were dedicated to the motives that would captivate him for the rest of his life. His interest in nature was probably laid in Günter Ziesler's cradle. Yet, only at the age of 34, did he make his hobby his profession to eventually be commissioned in 1977 by a Spanish publisher to take pictures on the national parks of South America for numerous illustrated books. In 1980, he met his co-worker and wife to be Angelika Hofer with whom he published the book "Safari", the result of a one-year trip through Kenya. The book appeared in six languages in an edition of 14,000 copies and is probably one of the best-known illustrated books on the nature wonders of Africa. However, South America remained his passion where he preferred to roam about in his camper. Especially, the tropical rain forest, the most difficult field for a photographer, caught his attention. His work influenced by Bengt Berg and other Scandinavian photographers like Hanu Hautula range in the contradictory context of dynamic flow and still life, whereby he is able to masterly impart an iconographic quality to all his pictures. In this way, a pair of lions in his photographs is given the status of a still life and a detail in a rain forest a dynamic radiance of a motion sequence. The preservation of the environment comes naturally to Ziesler. Since the year 2000, the exhibition "Abenteuer Regenwald" (Adventure Rain Forest), which he conceived together with Angelika Hofer, is touring schools and libraries in order to enhance public awareness of the ever-progressive destruction of the rain forests. To mention but a few, some important publications by Ziegler are "Ein Gänsesommer" (A Summer of the Geese), published in 1987 and one year later "Löwenkinderbuch" (Book of the Lion Children). In 1991, "Urwald-pfade" (Paths of the Primeval Forest), containing descriptions out of the South American rain forest, as well as the book "Mahale – Begegnungen mit Schimpansen" (Mahale – Encounters with Chimpanzees) were published. His latest work "Pantanal – das Herz Südamerikas" (Pantanal – the Heart of South America) was published in 2007.

Contact and Copyright Images:
Günter Ziesler
Am Riesenanger 7, 87629 Füssen, Germany
www.pan-photography.de

Impressum

Diese Publikation erscheint anlässlich der Ausstellung
«Wälder der Erde» im Magnum Verlag AG,
Arabienstrasse 5, CH-4059 Basel/Schweiz
Im Auftrag der gemeinnützigen Stiftung Wald-Klima-Umwelt

Erstausstellungsort
Fondation Beyeler
Baselstrasse 101, CH-4125 Riehen-Basel/Schweiz
Internet: www.beyeler.com
E-Mail: fondation@beyeler.com

Herausgeber
Stiftung Wald-Klima-Umwelt
Arabienstrasse 5, CH-4059 Basel/Schweiz
Internet: www.wald-klima-umwelt.ch
E-Mail: info@wald-klima-umwelt.ch
Tel.: +41 61 361 11 61
Fax: +41 61 361 06 61

© 2007 Magnum Verlag AG, CH-4059 Basel/Schweiz
© Bildrechte bei den Autoren oder deren Rechtsnachfolgern

ISBN 978-3-9523285-0-7
Gedruckt in der Schweiz

Lektorat/Übersetzung
Alexander Lukas Bieri
Rolf Steinebrunner

Gestaltung und Herstellung
Albert Gomm, Basel/Schweiz

Foto Umschlag
Günter Ziesler
Regenwald, Borneo/Malaysia

Fotovignetten Vorspann
Heinrich Gohl
Seite 2: Waldsilhouette, Grosser Wagen
Seite 6: Yukon-Mäander, Polarkreis, Alaska/USA
Seite 34: Hooper Bay, Alaska/USA

Fotovignetten Textteil
Heinrich Gohl
Seiten 16–33

Reproduktionen
Sturm AG, Muttenz/Schweiz

Satz und Druck
Birkhäuser+GBC AG, Reinach/Schweiz

Bindung
Schumacher AG, Schmitten/Schweiz

Exponate

Fototechnik
René Linder, Bremgarten/Schweiz

Einrahmungen
Philipp Mohler GmbH, Liestal/Schweiz

SARASIN

Hauptsponsor
Bank Sarasin, Basel/Schweiz

Gönner
Karl Mayer Stiftung
Ricola AG, Laufen/Switzerland

Masthead

The catalogue is published on the occasion of the exhibition
"Forests of the World" by Magnum Verlag AG,
Arabienstrasse 5, CH-4059 Basel, Switzerland
On behalf of the non-profit foundation Wald-Klima-Umwelt
(Forest-Climate-Environment)

First Site of the Exhibition
Fondation Beyeler
Baselstrasse 101, CH-4125 Riehen-Basel/Switzerland
Internet: www.beyeler.com
E-Mail: fondation@beyeler.com

Publisher
Stiftung Wald-Klima-Umwelt
Arabienstrasse 5, CH-4059 Basel/Switzerland
Internet: www.wald-klima-umwelt.ch
E-Mail: info@wald-klima-umwelt.ch
Tel.: +41 61 361 11 61
Fax: +41 61 361 06 61

© 2007 Magnum Verlag AG, CH-4059 Basel/Switzerland
© All rights reserved for the photographs by the
   photographers or their legal successors

ISBN 978-3-9523285-0-7
Printed in Switzerland

Editor/Translation
Alexander Lukas Bieri, Basel/Switzerland
Rolf Steinebrunner, Riehen/Switzerland

Design und Production Editing
Albert Gomm, Basel/Switzerland

Photography Cover
Günter Ziesler
Rain forest, Borneo/Malaysia

Photo Vignettes Prefix
Heinrich Gohl
Page 2: Wood silhouette, Big Dipper
Page 6: Youkon meander, Arctic Circle, Alaska/USA
Page 34: Hooper Bay, Alaska/USA

Photo Vignettes
Heinrich Gohl
Pages 16–33

Reproductions
Sturm AG, Muttenz/Switzerland

Prepress and Print
Birkhäuser+GBC AG, Reinach/Switzerland

Binding
Schumacher AG, Schmitten/Switzerland

The Exhibits

Photo Technique
René Linder, Bremgarten/Switzerland

Framing
Philipp Mohler GmbH, Liestal/Switzerland

SARASIN

Main Sponsor
Bank Sarasin AG, Basel/Switzerland

Patrons
Karl Mayer Stiftung
Ricola AG, Laufen/Switzerland